LeeAnn
Rawlins

Loving
Your
Husband
for Life

Creation House
Strang Communications Company
190 N. Westmonte Drive
Altamonte Springs, FL 32714
(407) 869-5005

to Willard,
my wonderful husband for twenty-four years,
whom I loved dearly

Acknowledgments

I want to express my gratitude to David Hazard, first my editor and then my friend. Without his encouragement, I probably would not have completed this project. The Lord used him as His servant to help me.

I would like to thank so many for their help and love which made this book possible:

Janice Rogers, for her words of encouragement to get me started on this project and to finish it.

Janet Benge, for the hours she put into this book both at the writing school we attended and in the first editing stage, and for her love and encouragement.

My friend Carolyn Bell and my sister Vevi Schrock, for the typing help they gave me in the first stages.

My son Lonnie, who gave me my first computer lessons. What a blessing!

My other two sons, Mark and Rob, who loved and encouraged me, and my many friends and family who did the same.

My dear husband, Duane, who gave me many constructive suggestions, stood by me and showed me God's faithfulness.

Most of all, my dear Lord Jesus, who prompted me to write this book and provided just the people I needed to help me complete it.

Contents

1

Love Never Ends

In 1984, Glynn "Scotty" Wolfe filed for his twenty-sixth divorce and began looking for his twenty-seventh bride. A former Hollywood stunt pilot with forty children, Wolfe was proud of his place in the *Guinness Book of World Records* as the most married man on earth.

According to Wolfe, seventy-six years old at the time, his latest marriage was failing because his thirty-eight-year-old wife was never at home. "These young women," he said, "don't want to stay home, wash and iron clothes and sweep the floor." Wolfe's casual attitude toward marriage is the epitome of today's society that enters and quits the union on the slightest provocation. It's little wonder that the sacredness of marriage has been largely lost, that about forty percent of all marriages end in divorce and that many more are terribly unhappy.

Even in Christian marriages, we tend to focus on our own self-interest, asking questions like: Should I give in on this point or fight for what I want? Should I look after myself before I look after him in this situation? If I give and keep on giving, will I be taken advantage of? And behind these questions is an even deeper one: Will I choose to love?

This question must be decided not just once while you're standing at the altar, but over and over every day. Your answer during the ups and downs, the good times and the bad, will determine whether you have a happy, solid marriage.

I'm writing primarily to women to show you the benefits of loving your husband. I'm speaking from my heart, telling you my personal experiences. One of my most painful was the sudden loss of my first husband, Willard, when he was just forty-three years old. As terrible as that day was, I recount it here because from it I learned one of the most important lessons in life.

Willard was raised on a farm in a beautiful valley near Eugene, Oregon. His family was Mennonite. Like a lot of the rural Mennonite boys, he left school after the eighth grade to go into farming.

What Willard lacked in formal education was more than made up for in practical wisdom—and a certain inner quality. You could call it integrity, because people who knew Willard would tell you he lived what he believed and was always true to his word. He soon gained the respect of farmers all over the valley. And he had a quiet kind of faith.

The kind of integrity people found in Willard can be seen in his relationship with an employee of ours named Walter. Walter started working for us when he was quite young, and then he went off to college. When he returned, he asked Willard for a full-time job. Willard saw great potential in Walter and wanted to hire him, but because we were just getting started ourselves, we couldn't afford to pay Walter a regular salary.

To get around this problem, Willard offered to hire Walter if he could pay him just once a year according to how our year had gone. Confident of Willard's integrity, Walter accepted that unusual arrangement, and twenty-some years later he's still paid that way.

I first met Willard at a church party. I'd come from Idaho to study at a Mennonite school. He was tall, handsome and athletic, with dark hair and a crooked grin. The first thing that attracted me, to be honest, was his quietness. He was almost shy.

As soon as we began to date, however, I saw at once how loudly his life spoke for what he believed. I'd been brought up with stability in a loving Christian home, and it was so important for me to see how much Willard respected his parents. He also loved church and attended regularly. I fell deeply in love with him. We were soon engaged, and a year later, in November 1960, we were married.

After our marriage, I continued to be impressed by Willard's respect for his parents. He was twenty at the time, and we were ready to strike out on our own. But out of respect for his father, he willingly honored the family custom that each son work at home until he turned twenty-one.

You would think that such an ideal-sounding young man and in-love young woman would have a perfect life together. No problems. No disagreements. In fact, I think we had a beautiful marriage, and it brought into this world three wonderful young men—our sons, Mark, Lonnie and Rob. But our marriage had its struggles. No marriage, no matter how ideal the spouses, is without its difficult times.

Learning to Love

Being in love is one thing, and learning to love is quite another.

We had a lot of learning to do in the twenty-four years we were married. I, especially, had many struggles in learning to adjust. You see, I have strong ideas about the way things should go. And even though I grew up in a Christian home, it was hard at first to allow Willard to be the leader in our marriage. It sounded like a good principle when I read it in the Bible, but it was so hard to practice!

On that Saturday morning in March 1984 when Willard told me he wasn't feeling well, it seemed to me we'd grown in many ways in a deeper spiritual unity. Willard was lying on the sofa in the den. He was tired and feeling a little weak. I thought it was the flu coming on, so I set a pot of chicken soup on the stove and continued to check on him as I went about my weekend cleaning routine.

As I worked, my mind was only half on my chores. My thoughts flitted to Willard, but I knew he'd be all right with a little rest and tender, loving care. I thought about the life we'd built here in western Oregon: a 2,500-acre grass-seed farm that sold to clients all over the world, a successful manufacturing firm and the house we'd designed and built ourselves.

I also thought about how we'd grown as a Christian couple. Not long before, we'd begun to read Scripture together, something I'd always wanted to do. We'd become quite sensitive to each other, and just that week, when Willard asked me to cancel some previous plans and spend Saturday at home with him, I could tell it was important to him. So I agreed.

When the soup was well cooked, I took the pot off the burner and poured a steaming bowlful. Carefully, I carried it into the den. There was Willard, still lying on the sofa—only this time there was a strange look in his eyes. I hesitated in the doorway. "Honey?"

"Oh!" he said, suddenly pressing his hands to his chest. "It hurts." Then his eyes closed and his head fell gently back.

There is no way to say exactly how intuitions come, but in the moment it took to set down the bowl and rush to Willard's side, I knew he was gone.

Rob, who had been playing table tennis with a friend in the family room, rushed to call a neighbor and an ambulance. I sat on the sofa, cradling my husband's head in my arms, praying and fighting the gripping pain.

Minutes later, the ambulance arrived and a team of emergency medical technicians tried to revive him. I stood next to Willard the whole time. One of the men, who was specially trained in cardiac emergencies, said it appeared that an aneurysm had burst in a major blood vessel near the heart. There had been no chance to save him.

In an instant's time, my husband was gone.

No Regrets

The emotions that surged over me in the days after Willard's death were amazing in some ways. The most overwhelming feeling, of course, was the pain. Over and over I prayed, "Please, God, it can't be true. He was so young. I loved him so much." But right in the midst of that pain was another feeling, a certain brightness of hope within. I can best explain it as a lack of regret.

One day, not long after Willard had left us, I was feeling very low. My son Rob was with me, and I began to cry. "If only I'd been with him all that morning," I said, "just sitting with him instead of cleaning the house."

"Mom," Rob replied, "that one day was not nearly as important to Dad as all the other days and years he knew you loved him."

Rob's words reminded me, assured me, of Willard's love for me. I truly had little to regret about our twenty-four years together. And, just as important to me, our children had little to regret about their mom and dad's marriage.

When you love, it fills your life with security and beauty. It spills over onto others around you—children, family, friends. The apostle Paul was certainly led of the Spirit when he wrote, "Love never fails" (1 Cor. 13:8). To put it another way, love overflows and goes on and on, blessing everyone it touches.

I have written this small book to encourage others to love their husbands for life. Without love, living with anyone is difficult at best. Love brings life. Perhaps you are living with a husband who doesn't meet your expectations. Maybe you don't feel a true unity with your man. Maybe you haven't yet realized how your love for your husband—or lack of it—affects your children. Yes, every aspect of your life can be influenced by the love you demonstrate in your marriage.

In all these areas, I can say that I've been blessed, not because I'm good, but because God is good. When He tells us to love, we can only follow His Word. He is ever present to help us in the difficult times.

He is the Lord of life and the Lord of love. He has encouraged me with a deep but simple truth about our marriage relationships, a truth on which this book is founded. It is simply this: You cannot lose by loving. Let me show you how His love in you can spill over and bless your entire life.

2

Expectations

I can still recall those first feelings of being in love. In fact, I remember gazing happily out the window of the office where I'd gotten my first job as a bookkeeper. It was a crisp November day, and I'd just told my handsome young farmer that I would marry him. It seemed as if all my dreams were coming true.

For years, I'd wanted to be married to a minister or a farmer. Now I'd found a man who loved the land, had a good business head on his shoulders and was a Christian who went to church. He seemed so solid in his beliefs. Willard didn't really talk about his faith like the other young men I'd dated, but I was sure that would change. After we're married, I thought, I'll just make a suggestion here and drop a hint there. I'll make some alterations.

Our wedding ceremony was beautiful, exactly according to all the careful plans I'd made. But after the wedding, my plan to make some alterations in Willard did not work at all. And goodness knows, I tried.

LOVING YOUR HUSBAND FOR LIFE

Trying to Change Him

For instance, I really wanted Willard to carry his Bible. I thought that if he didn't want to talk about his faith, at least he could show it with some outward sign. Other young men I'd dated carried their big, black, leather Bibles. I knew Willard had a real respect for God's Word, but I thought he should show it a little more. In my immaturity, I thought carrying your Bible was a sign of spirituality.

At first I dropped hints, like putting his Bible out on the table before church. All my hints fell flat. In fact, the more I hinted and the more persistent I became, the further it drove him from carrying his Bible. I knew Willard loved me. Why was he resisting in this one little thing?

For many years, I tried this same method of making suggestions about other things as well. I thought that if I kept making a suggestion, maybe Willard would eventually do it the way I thought best. But again and again, I found my suggestions falling flat.

Then one day, years after we were married, we heard about some special, spiritual-life meetings that were to be held at a nearby church. We knew and liked the speaker. Even though we often went to meetings of this kind, I somehow felt these meetings would be special. Yet when I suggested we go, Willard did not immediately say yes.

The morning of the first meeting, I was about to open my mouth and suggest that I make supper early so we could be on time for the church meeting, but something inside stopped me. I thought, This time I want to know that it's Willard's choice, not my prodding, that's behind his decision. If he doesn't want to go, or if he comes in from the fields tired, we'll just stay home.

So all that morning, I prayed. The feeling that these meetings were important did not go away, and I struggled with wanting to drop strong hints. But no, I decided I would not do that this time.

About noon, Willard came in for lunch. To my great surprise, he said, "Hon, I've been thinking about these meetings tonight. Let's plan to go."

I was thrilled, of course, but still kept quiet.

At suppertime, the boys seemed especially fussy. We had two little ones then, and it had been a tiring day with them. Now *I* was worn out. It would have been much easier to stay home. But I got the boys together, and off we went. Why was it so important to me to be at this meeting?

We arrived on time, and it proved to be a good service. But when it was over, I couldn't see why I'd felt it was so urgent for us to be there. It was only later, after we'd driven home and carried our sleeping boys to their beds, that it became clear.

Lying in bed that night, I was happy with the feeling of Willard's warmth beside me. In a few minutes, he said quietly, "I've decided to rededicate my life to Jesus. I want to give everything over to Him." My heart leaped. I gave him a tight hug, and tears of joy stung my eyes.

I knew then why it had been so important for us to be at church that night. And another thought occurred to me. I suddenly knew why it was so important that I not suggest and hint that Willard take us. If I had done

19

that, Willard might have resisted me and never been in the right place for the Holy Spirit to convict him of his need for a closer walk with the Lord.

Willard never did carry his Bible to church, though his spiritual life changed drastically. In terms of public ministry, he joined a gospel quartet, which eventually became a family-oriented ministry. At home, he became more open in sharing his thoughts with me, and we began to read the Bible together.

A New Perspective

Through the experience that night at the special church service, God taught me an important lesson about the expectations wives have for their husbands. It took me a long time to see that even before Willard committed his life totally to the Lord, he was the spiritual head of our home. There was such integrity about him. It was more than human pride; he believed in righteous living. He loved to give generously and in secret. He carefully chose where he would give our money so that it would be used wisely to the most benefit. As a father, he loved the boys and disciplined them firmly but fairly. And he loved me.

The funny thing was that once I saw more outward signs of his faith, I realized how deeply spiritual he'd been all along. But because he hadn't lived up to certain standards I'd set, he wasn't "spiritual" enough in my eyes.

That realization made me feel terrible. But there was something else that made me ashamed. All those years I'd dropped hints—and sometimes they were stronger than hints—I had actually driven Willard further away from the goal I really wanted!

When I stopped to ask God why I'd been that way, and why so many women I know badger their husbands, a verse came to mind: "Man looks at the outward appearance, but the Lord looks at the heart" (1 Sam. 16:7). I had assumed I knew what was going on in Willard's heart between him and the Lord. I'd been wrong.

Because I'd reacted to the outward evidence of Willard's faith, I'd been blind to other signs of his spirituality. So, fearing my husband wasn't spiritual, I prodded him with my helpful hints. The only result was that I caused him to react against me, and thus I undermined my whole plan. We can be so unaware of the harmful effects of our subtle pressure.

You may object immediately and say, "But I'm gentle in the things I suggest. My husband knows I love him, and I don't think I nag. Isn't he just being stubborn when he won't do something he knows I want?"

Many women struggle with these questions, because they don't know how men are motivated. A woman wants to be loved. She wants to feel she has a secure position at the center of a man's affections. A man also wants to be loved, but even more than that, he wants to be respected.

Once you understand this basic difference, you'll see how a nagging wife, or even a wife who drops subtle hints, can be hurting her relationship with her husband. In my case, I thought I was offering simple suggestions, wanting Willard to do certain things that would help him spiritually. But that wasn't all I was doing. My hints were saying to Willard, I don't accept you the way you are. You have to do such and such in order to be a better Christian in my eyes.

My focus was all wrong. For example, if you hold a coin in your fingers at arm's length, it looks small. You can clearly see other objects in the room around you. In fact, you might become interested in looking at something else and hardly notice the coin. But if you hold that coin up close to your eye, focusing on it intently, everything else in the room is concealed from your view. All you can see is the coin.

It's the same way for a woman who focuses in on one of her husband's flaws. Perhaps he's not making the kind of income she thinks he could, so she says he's lazy. He may be a good father and love his children. He may be a Christian with a heart that is fast after God. But because she's focused her eyes only on their financial struggle, she thinks of him as lazy.

Then the pressure begins. She comments casually, "It sure would be nice to be able to buy new furniture for the living room." "Every boy on the baseball team had a new glove, but I guess we can't afford to buy Junior one, can we, dear?"

While some men may give in to this kind of pressure, most will fight against it inwardly. It is not in their nature to be controlled by a wife's critical, unaccepting spirit. In fact, a husband may have one of several responses. He may become angry and resentful and pull away from his wife. He may simply look for affirmation elsewhere, either in his work or among male companions. In the worst case, a man may even turn to another woman.

In either case, a wedge is driven between them.

The Need for Respect

Am I saying that a woman has no power or influence in a marriage? Quite the opposite! Where a man has final authority, I believe a woman has final influence in the home. As you can see by the examples I've used, and by my own mistakes, a woman has a powerful impact. If she doesn't know that, or if she misuses it, she can bring great difficulties into her home. On the other hand, if she uses her influence wisely, she will bless her husband and her household.

The key is understanding what it means to respect your mate. In Ephesians 5, husbands are told to love their wives, and wives are told to *respect* their husbands. When you are critical, flaw-picking and unaccepting, you are not respecting your husband. You are focusing only on his weaknesses, not on his good points. In an unspoken way, you are treating him like a child who needs to be corrected.

I believe that when most adult men do something wrong they are aware it's wrong. Normally, you don't have to point out their mistakes. When you do, a man will wind up resisting you, and your point is lost. Or worse, the atmosphere of nonacceptance will build up into open fights.

On the other hand, when a wife responds positively to her husband, respecting him and complimenting his good points; something clicks on inside him. When a woman shows that she respects and trusts her husband, he wants to live up to that respect. He is greatly motivated to be even more of a man after God's design.

When this kind of support works in a marriage, you will stop the flow of negative forces at work between you and spur each other on with a positive, upbuilding power. Yes, we women can have godly influence in our homes. And as James says, our tongues have a great deal of power (see James 3).

Of course, I'm not just talking about what we say verbally. Our inner attitude must constantly be directed toward building up our husbands, because what we do—even the slightest look—can express feelings, thoughts and judgments.

I was talking recently with a young woman who was having trouble accepting some things about her husband. They were having minor disagreements, nothing overwhelming, but still she wanted a better marriage.

She practiced some of the points in this chapter: She stopped making comments aimed at redirecting him. She focused inwardly on his good points. Actually, she said very little.

Several weeks after she made this conscious choice to change her way of thinking about her husband, he confronted her one day. "What's going on?" he demanded, smiling. "Why do you suddenly seem to love me so much? It's as if we're on a second honeymoon. I don't know what I'm doing right these days, but I wish you'd tell me!"

I want you to stop and think for a moment: What do you *really* think of your husband? Does he live up to your expectations? Have you been trying to alter him? Have you tried to use subtle pressures and hints?

Start thinking now of his good points. *Tell* him about them. Make it a priority to tell him what you respect about him. Give him the freedom to be himself. Cheer him in his progress.

I guarantee that even if you already have a good marriage you will see improvements you never dreamed possible. You'll find that, as hard as you root for your mate, he'll be rooting for you, too. You'll feel as if your marriage is beginning all over again.

Even if God doesn't work miraculous changes in your husband right away, He will continue to give you the grace to accept and understand. Some husbands are hard to love. But God values them nonetheless. We women must give God the freedom and the time to work in our husbands' lives. When we stop complaining and start praying and loving, we are releasing God's Spirit to work in powerful ways.

Once we overcome our wrong expectations, we can experience a deeper level of marriage. It is the greatest blessing God has for us as husband and wife. I am speaking of becoming one in Christ.

3

Becoming One

W hat would bring the most fulfillment to your marriage? Having children? Establishing a family business? Building your dream house?

Often we replace the single most important goal in marriage, the thing essential to fulfillment in the relationship, with wrong goals. What will bring the most fulfillment is to become one with your husband. God intends for a husband and wife to become one. Genesis 2:24 says, ''A man will leave his father and mother and be united to his wife, and they will become one flesh.''

Today, unfortunately, a heavy emphasis is placed on independence. And an independent attitude is the very thing destroying so many marriages. Why did God institute marriage at all? Because two people, coming together in unity, can accomplish so much more together than either could accomplish alone. And in that unity, God demonstrates Himself to the world.

I found tremendous fulfillment in learning to work as a single unit with my husband. Willard was great at long-range planning, and I loved to help work out the details needed to reach those goals. But the responsibility for decision making was his, and that left me feeling liberated under his protection.

Smucker Manufacturing, the company we formed in 1980, is a good example of how we complemented each other when working together. It all started when Willard saw something at an agriculture show in California that gave him the idea for our first product—a more efficient way to apply weed killer to farm crops. Willard was great at seeing the potential in an idea and starting to make it practical. I, on the other hand, with my orientation toward details, served as the travel agent, researcher, accountant and executive secretary. Together we built a thriving business.

How do you build oneness between you and your husband? Many of us come into a relationship and immediately set boundaries and limitations. We say, "I'll do this, but only if you promise to do that." We want to have tight control over relationships, and the underlying reason is *fear*: We fear we will be taken advantage of or used. And when we fear, we cannot love freely.

Becoming a Servant

The first step in becoming one with your husband is to take on the attitude of a servant. Philippians 2:2 says, "Live together in love, as though you had only one mind and one spirit between you" (Phillips). That means you are to love your husband as you would love yourself, to do for him what you would want done for yourself. Selfishness disrupts unity and destroys happiness. If you want to love as a servant, you cannot take the position that it's your husband's responsibility to make you happy. Instead, take the position that it's your responsibility to make him happy. Give yourself to make him happy. Luke 6:38 says, "Give and men will give to you" (Phillips).

When you give to someone, he can't help but give back to you. That's the beauty of taking on the attitude of a servant.

The Challenge of Submission

Another position you must take if you want unity and happiness with your husband is to submit to his authority. I realize many women today get upset when they hear these words, but that's because submission has not been properly understood. In contemporary usage, to be in submission implies inferiority. This usage bears little resemblance, however, to the biblical meaning of the word. Even among Christians, the concept has been misunderstood and applied wrongly. Consequently, many Christian women have felt justified in disobeying God on this principle.

Nonetheless, submission is a biblical principle, and its proper application is another step in building true unity in marriage. Ephesians 5:21-24 says, "Submit to one another out of reverence for Christ. Wives, submit to your husbands as to the Lord. For the husband is head of the wife as Christ is the head of the church, his body, of which he is the Savior. Now as the church submits to Christ, so also wives should submit to their husbands in everything."

The first thing to note about this passage is that it is honoring to Christ when we submit to our husbands.

This is emphasized by the apostle Paul's statement, "Wives, submit to your husbands, as is fitting in the Lord" (Col. 3:18).

Second, we recognize that God has ordained a certain family structure. In every organization, there must be a president or a leader who makes the decisions; otherwise, there would be endless disputes. This final authority, which I mentioned in the previous chapter, was given by God to men, not that they should belittle women or ignore their thoughts and feelings, but that there should be order.

In this submitted position, however, the wife has ample room for expressing her feelings, hopes and desires, and for helping her husband think through a plan of action on any given issue. Feminists often say the Bible gives men permission to run roughshod over their wives or even mistreat them. But men are to love their wives. The Bible does not say or even imply that a man should treat his wife as though she were mentally inferior. When it comes time to make the final decision, however, that must be left up to the man. This is the order God has chosen.

When a woman wrests this position from her husband in any way, she is bringing destruction upon her own home. She can do it in numerous ways. She can belittle him and his choices in front of his friends, colleagues or, even worse, his own children. She can allow him to think she's going along with him and then turn around and handle things her own way.

Each of these approaches shows rebelliousness, and each brings confusion and disruption into a home. This independent attitude quickly destroys unity, communication and love. Women who undercut their husbands don't realize how far-reaching are the effects of their actions. In our family business, we have employed many men as day laborers. Again and again, we saw the influence a wife has on her husband, for better or for worse.

When I think of women who support their husbands, I immediately think of the wives of two men who work for us. Sheila is always lively and on top of things, encouraging her husband, Ben, every step of the way. And there is Dot, who trusts the decisions of her husband, Walter, and stands behind him always. There is an enormous difference in the workplace between men like Ben and Walter and some others who worked for us in the past. These men are happy and have peace and confidence because they are built up and supported at home.

Giving God the Front Seat

A third position we must take if we want spiritual oneness with our husbands is to take a backseat to God. When we become tense and upset about something our husbands are doing or failing to do, we're really showing a lack of faith in God. Sometimes—even much of the time—we must relinquish our husbands into God's hands. Surely we can trust our heavenly Father to work out a plan that is best, not only for our husbands, but also for us.

As a young woman I thought there could be nothing greater than to marry a farmer or a minister. (And I thought, If I could find a man who is both, I'll be happy forever.) Well, I got my farmer, but the part about the minister didn't come with the package—at least not right away. God had some work to do in Willard, and I had to learn how to walk by faith and not by sight (see 2 Cor. 5:7).

When we were first married, I'd wanted to attend a certain church in our area. Willard wasn't ready to make a change, so he wouldn't budge. I kept hinting that we try it out, but eventually—for once!—I felt I should leave it up to God to work in Willard's heart. After all, at least I had a husband who wanted to go to church, whereas a lot of women didn't!

After we'd been married about six years, Willard came to me one day and said, "I feel that God is leading me to take our family to a different church." And guess which one he suggested! If I thought that was the answer to my prayers, however, I was in for a big surprise.

Soon after we became established in our new church home, Willard was invited to sing with three other men in a gospel quartet. The group was to do an occasional special song during a church service. He accepted.

Shortly after the group started, their ministry expanded. Not only were they performing regularly in our church, but others also heard about the special sound these four men could produce and the fact that they gave a powerful testimony in music. Before long, they were singing in other churches in the area.

Eventually, this quartet grew and drew in the families of each of the men involved. Soon we were known as the Good Shepherd Quartet and Families. Our own children were just little when we began. But as they grew, they and some of the other children formed a backup band for the singers. For eighteen years, we traveled to churches all over the Northwest, encouraging others to serve the Lord.

Being a part of the Good Shepherd Quartet and Families was an unforgettable experience for us all. It molded our sons in the service of the Lord and gave them spiritual insights into the needs of people at an early age. So my dream of having a farmer who was a minister came true as I relinquished my plans to the Lord. More than that, our whole family was blessed as we grew in faith together. And through it all, Willard and I grew into a deep unity as husband and wife.

I sometimes shudder to think what would have happened if I had begged and pleaded and nagged Willard about taking me to the church where I wanted to go before he was ready. Of course, I know things don't always turn out exactly as we hoped, and I can't promise you the fulfillment of every one of your desires, for not all of mine have been fulfilled. But I do know that God desires for husbands and wives to become one flesh. And sometimes this means letting go of our dreams to let God fulfill them in His way and in His timing. Along the way, as was the case in our home, I know He will answer your prayers beyond your wildest imaginings.

It is no small thing that Proverbs, the greatest book of wisdom on earth, closes with words of praise for the godly woman. She works constantly to serve her husband, to submit to him, and she constantly relinquishes him in prayer to God. In the words of Solomon, "Charm is deceptive, and beauty is fleeting; but a woman who fears the Lord is to be praised. Give her the reward she has earned, and let her works bring her praise at the city gate'' (Prov. 31:30-31).

When a woman gives herself to her husband, first in service and then in submission, a transformation will take place in that marriage. The woman who chooses this path to unity with her husband need not fear that she will be made to give and keep on giving while her husband takes no notice. For when a man senses this kind of unselfish love, when he feels the unqualified support of his wife, he will turn to her and say, ''What can I do to make you happy?''

Yes, no matter how much in love a couple may be when they are first wed, they are still two minds, two personalities, two souls. It takes a lot of work and love to become one. But the rewards of unity are beyond compare. Then, when we have laid aside our independence and learned to walk in unity, we'll find that the man who walks at our side will become our greatest friend on earth.

4

Making a Marriage Sparkle

Some women dream of keeping that special sparkle in their marriages forever. But most, I'm afraid, let go of that dream after the first couple of years of married life. "A sparkling marriage?" they retort. "Maybe for newlyweds. But after a while—well, it's just unrealistic. The sparkle wears off for everyone."

Think for a moment about the early days of your marriage. If you were already home when he came in from work, can you recall the joy of his homecoming? Did you ever wake up before he did and just lie there, studying his face, loving to look at him? Willard and I were in love like this. And I can recall the moment, some years after we were married, when I first noticed that the sparkle had dimmed. It was a difficult day.

We were expecting guests for the weekend. I was getting clean sheets out of the linen closet—the good linens, of course, for the visitors. As I slid the sheets off the shelf, I had a sinking feeling. Gone was their pure-white crispness. They looked washed out and limp. Suddenly, I noticed other signs of wear that I'd overlooked until then: a chip in the pretty rose china we'd been given as a wedding gift and a dent one of the boys had made in the wooden table top. Not that possessions mattered much to us, but their worn look called my attention to something far more important.

We were in our ninth year as husband and wife—nine happy, blessed years. We had two healthy boys and a new home. We loved each other. Then why did I feel further from Willard than I had before we were married? No, that wasn't quite it. But we just didn't seem close. Like the dull sheets and the chipping china, our marriage seemed to have lost its fresh newness.

Mentally, I took a half-panicked inventory. Had Willard changed? Was it I? Had we taken each other for granted? Was our marriage going wrong? I hated the feeling that we had lost something forever, that it had slipped from our fingers without our notice.

We used to love to spend as much time together as possible. Even when Willard was working long hours on the combine during harvest season, I rode with him as often as possible. Of course, that changed when the boys came along. I had to give them as much time as possible, I reasoned.

In the days following my initial panic, I searched my heart and watched our relationship. By that I mean I observed what we were like when we were with each other. It was awful. We could be in the same room, looking at each other, talking to each other—and I still had the terrible sense that we were not communicating. This was true even when the children weren't in the room and we could talk without interruption. I felt that something inside me was not touching the inside of him.

With that came the terrible doubts. Maybe we'd outgrown each other somehow. Maybe he felt it, too. We had even become haphazard about kissing good-bye in the morning when he left for work. And what if he started to look elsewhere—to his work or to hobbies, perhaps—for the fulfillment he used to find in being with me?

So we did what many people do when they feel their marriage needs rejuvenating: we had another baby!

Our third son, Rob, was an adorable baby. He won our hearts instantly. What's more, it was such fun to have a new baby again. And just as I'd hoped, things were better between Willard and me—for a while.

In spite of our happiness with Rob, our marriage did not improve. Before long, we were back in the same rut, almost living separate lives under one roof. Are any of these feelings familiar? Whether you feel your marriage has lost its sparkle or is still shining brightly, I want to tell you what we learned about keeping the sparkle in our marriage.

Maintaining Togetherness

It was near our tenth anniversary, and I was still feeling unsettled and helpless. By this time, I knew Willard was as aware of the problem as I was. Then he made a decision that changed our marriage.

He came into the kitchen one evening, looking tired after a hard day in the fields. He would always hug me, but this time he held me in his arms and looked me in the eyes. "Hon, we need to get away together," he said with a smile. "Just you and me."

My first response inwardly was, Oh, no! What about

our little boys? And the baby? They need me! How could my children survive without Mommy? ''Why don't we take the kids with us?'' I suggested.

Willard's smile faded.

It took me some time to work through my feelings about leaving the boys so that I could be alone with my husband. As a Christian parent, I'd been taught to devote a lot of time to my children. I loved my boys. How I wanted to be a good mother!

In the end, we left the boys in capable hands and took a short trip to San Francisco. We didn't have a lot of money to spend, but that didn't matter, because it was a major turning point for our marriage.

I can still recall the hilly streets with their cable cars, and the romantic dinner overlooking the bay. Willard surprised me with a new ring! I felt so special. But the most special part was that I could see Willard cared about us. We were together again in ways we had not been together in a long, long time.

This was just the beginning of a new relationship. Everything didn't change overnight. It took lots of work and time. But a door opened, and we began to talk honestly with each other. Some things we said hurt, but the hurt was healthy, because it was wrapped in the solid commitment of our love.

How do you keep the sparkle in your marriage? The first thing we learned is to take time for one another. Even though you pass the time doing the same things— eating at the same table, sitting side-by-side on the sofa watching television or sleeping in the same bed—it doesn't mean you are spending time together.

When you have children, your time together gets cut drastically. Certainly, in the early months of a baby's life, Mom's constant nurturing care is necessary. But too often, women continue to feel their children's total dependency long after it is necessary. I'm not suggesting you neglect your children. But there's a time for that intense nurturing, and there's a time to take on the role of a wife again. I am not speaking just of the physical relationship, but also of the time and attention it takes to keep a marriage alive.

Later we'll look more at the effects of a good marriage on children. For now, I want to emphasize that becoming a mother doesn't mean you have to give up being a wife. One of the hurtful things I learned as Willard and I began to communicate again was that it seemed to him as if I'd stopped caring. He was working hard to make our farm succeed, and he felt I was spending all my efforts on the boys. He was mostly right.

You can show your husband you care in lots of little ways. It doesn't take a huge effort, a lot of time or money. It can mean fixing his favorite meal or surprising him with a candlelit dinner out. (A wife doesn't have to wait for her husband to ask her on a date, after all!) A small thing I did was to put little notes in Willard's lunch on occasion. You can be as creative as you'd like.

Once, around the time of Willard's birthday, I was trying to think of something special to give him. I didn't want to get him another tie or bottle of cologne. Then an idea came—I'm sure it was from the Lord, because I'm not that creative. I would get a simple, inexpensive notebook, and each day from then until his next birthday, I'd write down something about him that made me love him.

For 365 days, I kept that love journal. What a joy it was to take time each day to turn to that little notebook! I have to be honest and say there were some days when I just couldn't find anything positive to write. (Those days were few, fortunately.) Then I'd read what I'd written on one of the earlier days. This turned into a great blessing for me. And as the months passed and Willard's birthday approached, my anticipation grew.

I will never forget the look in Willard's eyes when he unwrapped my precious little book on his birthday. He chuckled at my honesty when I told him about the blanks. And he was greatly moved to read about himself as seen through my eyes.

For any of these ideas to be effective requires some effort. Whether your demonstration of love is elaborate or simple, it is most effective when it shows you are sensitive to your husband's needs, his likes and dislikes. In this, I learned to watch for unspoken responses as well as spoken. I learned to pick up on small comments dropped in casual conversation and to watch his facial responses in order to read his moods. (I told you Willard was not a talker, so it wasn't always easy to know what was going on inside him.)

Am I giving you the impression that effective communication with someone you love is hard work? Then you're reading me loud and clear! When you zero in on your husband's personality, interests and needs, he can't help but be affected and return the consideration.

Building Trust

Some men feel they cannot trust their wives. I don't mean they're suspicious, but they're concerned about trustworthiness in a way most women don't even consider.

It's difficult for many men to express their private thoughts and emotions as it is. This is just the way some men are, and wishing it were otherwise won't change things. But when a man shares something intimate, he expects complete confidence. He wants to know you can be trusted. But sometimes when a husband talks about emotions he senses that his wife is telling them to her best friend.

This is true of many women. Unfortunately, it is most true of Christian women. Sometimes we Christian women share intimate things about our spouses in prayer groups. We pick up the phone and call a close sister in the Lord. Or we may seek out our pastors. Not all of what is said should be said. More than that, the more a woman relies on others to be her confidantes, the less she needs her husband's confidence.

So if you want to see the luster stay in your marriage or return, be your husband's confidante. Be trustworthy with the feelings and secrets he has entrusted to you.

Don't Neglect the Physical

Yet another reason marriages lose their sparkle is that couples neglect their sexual relationship. And while I want to address that, for several reasons I'm not going to get explicit with suggestions for helping your sex life.

First, what works for one couple may not work for another. Second, it's so important that you learn what pleases *your* man. And third, it will improve your communication greatly to learn about him in this realm of intimacy. The sexual relationship is such an important part of marriage. But couples, especially those who have been together for years, can become dangerously neglectful of each other.

Therapists say that a poor sex life is often a symptom of deeper problems and that solving those problems will improve sexual relations. There is a lot of truth to that, of course. But sex is too important a part of the marital mix to assume it is merely a symptom that will take care of itself when other problems are solved. That is not true. Sex is a building block for constructing and maintaining a solid, happy marriage. A good sexual relationship can keep a marriage together when a lot of other things are shaky.

Closely related to the sexual aspect of marriage is physical appearance. Remember when you and your husband were first seeing each other? You probably went to great lengths to look appealing, trying to wear the most flattering clothes. Do you still hold that attitude, or are you neglectful of your appearance?

Ladies, we need to look the best we can for our husbands. You need not spend lots of time each day, but take a few minutes to fix your hair and put on a tasteful touch of makeup and clothes that are neat and becoming. It requires such little effort, really, and I guarantee your husband will appreciate it. You'll also feel better about yourself, and that will make you feel better about him, too.

You might even have your husband help you pick out clothes. If he doesn't like to shop, you can always ask his opinion about the styles he likes to see you wear. You can show him pictures in a catalog or model your purchases for him.

Some women feel they have a right to look the way they want. They consider makeup and choice of clothing their business. I had a mind of my own in all these matters, but I needed to know what Willard liked and to live up to his best picture of me. He was delighted when he saw that I tried to please him in this.

Showing Respect

Along with caring, trust, sexuality and your appearance, there is one other crucial principle of marriage. It can break a relationship or make it shine. I am referring to the respect and admiration we show to our husbands. Ephesians 5:33 says, "And the wife must respect her husband."

One of the most important things we need to learn in this area is control of our words. Proverbs 18:21 says, "The tongue has the power of life and death." That means your words can bring life to your husband and marriage, or they can tear down and destroy both.

How do you apply this wise proverb? You don't have to be fawning and complimenting your man all the time. But consider this: Do you fly off the handle and say terrible, destructive things when you're angry, or do you try to give a soft answer? A harsh reply will make him defensive; a soft reply will allow him to change his mind without being threatened. Do you belittle him when he's made a mistake or hurt you? Encouraging him to try again, telling him you know he can succeed, will make him strong. Do you take for granted the long hours he works to support the family? Thanking him will build up his spirit and self-esteem and can make his job seem more worthwhile, no matter how difficult it is. Does he only hear your complaints, or does he sometimes hear, "I'm glad I married you"?

Proverbs 3:27 says, "Do not withhold good from those who deserve it." When your husband deserves encouraging, loving words from you, don't hold back. Make it a practice to speak love and admiration in your home.

Another aspect of admiration that goes deeper than words is how you think about your husband. It's important to establish an attitude of acceptance. In 1 Corinthians 13:5, Paul said, "Love...does not keep account of evil" (Phillips). Some women keep long accounts of the irritating or hurtful things their husbands did, do and probably will do. They become seething volcanoes of anger and resentment, and when that anger has worked deep and long enough, it becomes depression.

It's obvious that any two people who live together are going to hurt and anger each other. That's the way life is. The secret of keeping an admiring spirit is to have a forgiving heart. The longer you store away moldy, old hurts and petty gripes, the more they will rot away your respect for your husband.

I learned to make a spiritual housecleaning of my thoughts regularly. This always re-established an attitude of admiration in me for my husband. Goethe, the

German author, said, "If you treat a man as he is, he will stay as he is. But if you treat him as if he were what he ought to be and could be, he will become that bigger and better man." If you believe your man is a good husband, you will talk as if he's a good husband. Then you will treat him as if he's a good husband, and he will become a good husband. Affirmation and love unlock the door to a warm, sparkling marriage.

A final word about admiration: A wife needs to act admiringly toward her husband. Some women today have an independent, I-don't-need-a-man's-help sort of attitude. But depending on your husband for help will appeal to his manly attributes. Ask him to help you with heavy objects and difficult tasks. Seek his opinion, and rely upon him as the final authority in your home. This attitude will appeal to something deep inside him that wants to shepherd and protect.

Keep Praying

The most important thing you can do to add sparkle to your marriage is to pray. Man's answer to problems is to try to solve them on his own. We women, even Christian women, can get caught up in this same behavior when it comes to trying to handle marital problems. When our efforts fail and our husbands don't change, we become frustrated. Frustration usually leads to nagging. Proverbs 21:19 says, "Better to live in a desert than with a quarrelsome and ill-tempered wife." We women don't like to hear that, but it's true.

Ladies, we cannot solve marital frustrations on our own. God wants us to pray. Prayer does change things.

Nagging is a pretty good sign that you're not praying or that you're praying with wrong motives. We pray, "Oh, God, change this, that and the other about my husband." God knows your husband's sins and flaws. That doesn't mean you shouldn't confess your hurts to God. But when you do, allow Him to heal them. And above that, what He wants you to pray for is mercy and blessing for your husband. In this kind of prayer, a wife is released from a nagging spirit. She can trust God to do what she cannot. Even the hardest heart can be softened through prayer.

I realize that some husbands are hard to love. So often today, women want to bail out of a difficult relationship before they have even tried to make it work. We must each realize that God loves our husbands so much more than we can or do. Your man is of infinite worth to God, just as you are. Knowing that God values your husband makes your efforts worthwhile.

When you practice the things discussed here, you will find that Philippians 2:2 becomes a reality in your marriage. Remember what the apostle Paul wrote: "Live together in harmony, live together in love, as though you had only one mind and one spirit between you" (Phillips). What a joy to be two, yet one!

Begin today to rekindle the fires of godly love between you and your husband. Do away with the attitudes, sinful actions and words that tarnish your relationship. With God's help, you can keep the sparkle in your marriage!

5

Love and Friendship

Important as it is to keep the sparkle in your marriage, a wife can sometimes overlook an even more basic goal: Make your husband your friend, and make yourself his *best* friend. Nothing could better describe the love we want to have for our husbands than these words from the apostle Paul:

> This love of which I speak is slow to lose patience—it looks for a way of being constructive. It is not possessive: it is neither anxious to impress nor does it cherish inflated ideas of its own importance. Love has good manners and does not pursue selfish advantages. It is not touchy. It does not keep account of evil or gloat over the wickedness of other people. On the contrary, it is glad with all good men when truth prevails. Love knows no limit to its endurance, no end to its trust, no fading of its hope; it can outlast anything. It is, in fact, the one thing that still stands when all else has fallen....In this life we have three great lasting qualities—faith, hope and love. But the greatest

of them is love (1 Cor. 13:4-8, 13, Phillips).

Love is commitment, both to God and to a person. When we make this commitment, we're saying, "I will give you true love. And when I don't feel like it, I will give until I do feel like it."

Most Americans marry for love, but that word means to them nothing like the definition Paul gave it. To most contemporary Westerners, love equals sexual attraction and a warm feeling inside. No wonder our media depict love as something beyond our control. It is here today and gone tomorrow. When it's here, get married; when it's gone, get divorced.

Even Christians who can recite 1 Corinthians 13 by heart are still tainted by the world's brand of love. We often apply Paul's words to complete strangers and yet forget to apply them to those closest to us. I know I have had trouble with this.

For instance, if Willard or one of the boys walked over a freshly waxed floor, I might hit the ceiling. But if a neighbor accidentally walked in, my reaction was different. I might not even mention the fact that they were ruining my hard work. I concealed my reaction because I wanted to be polite, and that was *really* hard work.

Working at Friendship

Why don't we connect the words *work* and *love*? True, committed love, the basis for a strong friendship, is work. You can fall into love (that is, infatuation), but you do not fall into friendship. You build friendship through shared experiences and through learning to

48

trust. Friends share dreams and celebrate successes without being jealous. They are nonjudgmental, yet they can point out when you're making a fool of yourself. Friends compliment and enjoy the reward of a grateful smile. They relax with each other because of the atmosphere of sincere, unconditional acceptance.

Isn't this the kind of friendship you want with your husband? Isn't it worth working for?

There's another reason you should make it a priority to win and keep your husband's friendship: It may be that your husband does not have a friend. And it's certain that no one in the world can be as true and loyal a friend as you.

Alan Loy McGinnis, in *The Friendship Factor*, says that some of America's leading psychologists and therapists were asked how many men ever have real friends. Most guessed that as few as *ten percent* of American males enjoy close friendships with anyone. What a grim picture!

With this sad statistic in mind, let me ask: Isn't it wise for a woman to take the initiative to cultivate friendship with her husband? If you make a concentrated effort to understand and meet the needs of your mate, I promise you will find the dearest pal of your life. How do we build this life-long kind of friendship that is so necessary to a wonderful marriage? Earlier, we talked briefly about giving attention to the things that interest your husband. Showing this kind of interest is one of the most important things you can do to build a foundation of love.

I can already hear some of you groaning! I know what

you're thinking: But I hate football. I don't enjoy talking about politics. Money matters and talk about investments don't interest me in the least.

I know exactly what you mean. One of the things my husband and sons most enjoyed on Sunday afternoons was going to fish hatcheries. Somehow that was not a turn-on for this mother. I tried to reason with myself that they worked long, hard hours on the farm and deserved this enjoyment; that they had at least chosen an activity on which I could go along. But my inner response remained the same: Fish hatcheries, no less!

I forced myself to go along grudgingly—until I realized the effect my unwillingness had. I was dampening their joy and ruining my own Sunday afternoon. It was then I decided to change things. I brought along a book or some stationery so I could write a letter while Willard and the boys watched the fish. If the weather was nice, I'd bring a blanket and sunbathe.

It wasn't long before *I* began to enjoy our Sunday outings. And it became clear to me that the reason for my change of attitude was that I'd made a choice. I learned you can make almost anything pleasant or unpleasant depending on your attitude. I even came to enjoy, not just trips to the hatcheries, but fishing trips as well.

I guess you've caught on that fishing was a big deal in our family. I really wanted to like to fish, but hard as I tried, I could never enjoy standing on a river bank and swatting mosquitoes while holding a pole with a dying worm on a hook! Yet I decided to apply this directive from Philippians 2:4, which I'll reproduce from the

Amplified Bible: "Let each of you esteem and look upon and be concerned for not (merely) his own interests, but also each for the interests of others." If this was how Willard got his kicks, I decided I'd find something good about it.

The truth is that the only thing I found good about fishing was the company. But that was enough to make it enjoyable, both for me and for Willard.

The consequence of not working at mutual interests is too costly. When you make up your mind that your shared interests are few and you might as well go your separate ways, you've come to a fork in the road. From then on, you will grow further apart as friends. Eventually, you'll end up with a huge wall between you. Like too many people today, you may hear yourself complaining to your pastor or to a marriage counselor, "We just don't have anything in common anymore."

Giving yourself unselfishly to him and his interests will reverse this destructive tendency to pull apart. Our God is inventive, and you can ask Him for ideas to help you bridge the chasm of silence between you and your husband. God will help you take interest in your husband's work, hobbies and habits. He will help you study your husband and know what makes him angry, amused, bored, happy, discouraged or pleased. And the more you know him, the more your interest will thrill him.

Dealing With Disappointments

At the same time, I know that many women wish their husbands would pay attention to *their* interests. This, too, is important to building your friendship, since a good relationship is never one-sided. But I must offer a word of caution: Too often, we have high expectations, and when they aren't met, our hopes can be dashed. Then our relationships suffer badly, because we go about in stony silence, or else we pout. The cure for the sulks is to be flexible.

It took many big disappointments (and many days of tearful pouting, I'm embarrassed to say) for me to learn this basic lesson of flexibility. I was a great planner and loved to work out the details of a date with Willard long in advance. Eventually, our plans together became less and less frequent. Willard would also spring things on me, such as an evening out now and again, which I found out I did not enjoy. I was growing frustrated. Finally, I brought up the issue with him. I didn't like what I discovered.

To my surprise, I found that he preferred to plan our dates together, too. But he had stopped making plans with me because too often something came up to intervene, and then I would be terribly disappointed. As I said, I'd pout. So he learned not to promise anything, and that way he didn't have to deal with my disappointment. The alternative was to plan things on the spur of the moment, when he knew they would work out, even if neither of us liked it that way. All because of my reaction!

One time, for example, we had planned a much-needed vacation after the fall harvest. As I recall, we were going to go to Australia, and we figured we needed three weeks to do the trip right. But as the time neared, we both came to the conclusion that we couldn't afford to be away from our business for so long just then. I knew that canceling our plans was the right decision, but I still found it hard to accept and didn't hide my disappointment.

At the root of my pouting was selfishness. When I looked beyond my own feelings, I realized Willard had often been disappointed, too, when plans didn't work out. I'd been too wrapped up in my own emotions to notice.

I also had to learn flexibility in our communication. Clear communication is another foundation stone of friendship. Unfortunately, husbands and wives don't always express their hopes and needs clearly.

As I've mentioned several times, Willard was a man of few words. When he spoke, his words were genuine and often full of wisdom. On the other hand, I have always been full of words—brimming over! This created a stress in our marriage. You see, like so many women, I needed to hear those special words, "I love you." And I wanted to hear them often. But I didn't, so I wound up being hurt.

Once, when I told Willard about my hurt, he said, "If I tell you I love you as often as I know you want me to, I'm afraid the words will lose their meaning. I want it to be worth something when I say I love you." I agreed with him, but it didn't take away my need to hear those words. So we worked out a little plan. When I needed to know he loved me, I would ask, "Do you?" And he would smile and simply say, "Yeah." That may sound a little silly, but it worked for us.

Staying Transparent

Another stone in the foundation of friendship is transparency—that is, the willingness to be open with each other about your innermost feelings and responses.

A popular saying not long ago was, "Love means never having to say you're sorry." *No way.* Love means saying you're sorry over and over and over if necessary! And it means being able to bring up the things that hurt you.

Many Christians have the mistaken idea that they should never tell their mates—or anyone else—about things that hurt them. Somehow we think it's wrong to be offended, or we're too proud to admit we're still human and our feelings get bruised. Maybe we've grown up believing it's important to have "peace at any price." So we hide our feelings away—at least we think we're hiding them.

Something happens, however, when we try to conceal our emotions. Even if we think we've forgotten offenses, they keep storing up inside us. And then a small incident rubs us the wrong way, and it touches off an emotional explosion. The other person is left staring at us and wondering if we've gone off the deep end!

For others, this kind of explosion may never occur. We may be good at holding our tongues when we'd like to express anger or bitterness. The problem is that we may hold our tongues but express hostility in the way we act. Buried anger can lead to depression, physical and emotional coldness toward our husbands, or actions that are subtly aimed at hurting them.

The Bible gives the best solution for handling these

emotions: "Do not let the sun go down while you are still angry" (Eph. 4:26). Some have called this keeping short accounts. The principle is to deal with hurts as soon as possible, before they bury themselves in your spirit and become depression, bitterness or rage. Don't let bitterness destroy friendship with your spouse. Take the initiative to seek forgiveness or to build bridges where the relationship has been damaged.

I learned an important lesson in this regard from a dear friend named Linda, whom I came to know and love through the Good Shepherd Quartet and Families ministry. One time, Linda did something that caused me to take offense. When she found I was offended, she came to me and said, "I didn't mean that the way you took it." Then the next thing she said changed the way I've viewed friendships ever since. She said, "Don't you know that I love you too much to hurt you intentionally? Please remember that the next time I do something that offends you."

Sooner or later, every friend will do something that offends or hurts, especially the friend who lives the closest. Perhaps more than learning how to express our hurts, we need to take less notice of them. We need to tolerate errors, to see them as the result of human frailty and show the same kind of forgiving grace God shows when He covers our sins and faults. Hebrews 12:15 says, "Watch out that no bitterness takes root among you, for as it springs up it causes deep trouble, hurting many in their spiritual lives" (TLB). The best antidote for bitterness is the kind of grace I've been describing.

As we cultivate this attitude of grace, it will become

easier to be transparent about our positive feelings. Affirming your husband will build that strong friendship you desire. This is so important in a marriage—and so seldom done—that I want to emphasize it. When you affirm each other with true sincerity, you will build a bond of friendship such as you never thought possible. Words are tools—use them to build, not to tear down. Affirm, and your friendship will grow.

One often-overlooked area when it comes to transparency is being open in your appreciation of your husband's character and what he does for you. Too often, a woman fails to express her appreciation, to her detriment.

An extreme case, perhaps, is that of a woman I know. She's something of a perfectionist, and early in her marriage, when her husband would buy her gifts, she always found that they weren't quite "right." Perhaps the color was a shade off; perhaps it wasn't just the right, up-to-the-minute design. There was inevitably some reason to take the gift back and exchange it for something of her own choosing. Eventually, her husband gave up. When she spoke to me about her situation, she mournfully wished she had never criticized but had expressed appreciation—for now she has to buy and even wrap her own Christmas presents if she wants something under the tree! Her husband refuses to shop for her at all.

When you express appreciation for a man and what he does for you, it's more than likely you'll see one important result: He will love to do good things for you. Nothing brings about good results like reward.

Singing His Praises

One more foundation stone on which your friendship with your husband can be made solid is honoring him before others. In Proverbs 31, the godly wife is portrayed as one whose husband is "known in the city gates." By this, Solomon meant that her husband is respected in the community based on his wife's reports about him.

Think about this for a moment: Would your husband's friends, family and brothers and sisters in Christ respect him because of your reports about him? Or do they mostly know his flaws and perhaps even hidden sins because of your "sharing"?

Every once in a while, when Willard was on a trip, he would run into someone who knew me but had not met him before. It was so gratifying to me when he would come home from one of these chance meetings, beaming from ear to ear, and say, "This person told me, 'From all that LeeAnn has said about you, I can hardly wait to get to know you. You must be a remarkable man.' "

To so many people, you are your husband's only representative. How do you represent him? I so much wanted to set my husband apart, to have people respect him for the man he was. This has two beautiful results. First, good reports have a way of getting back to the person you've complimented. Second, when you love and respect someone in this way, you can be sure he will speak lovingly of you.

After Willard's death, a friend who had gone with him on a fishing trip to Alaska called on me one day.

He told me that one evening, as they were sitting around the campfire with their guide, Willard got up and went into the tent. The guide then turned to our friend and said, "That Willard sure is a quiet one. But one thing I know about him, he really loves his wife!"

I will probably never know, this side of eternity, exactly what good things Willard said about me to that stranger. But I know that if I were in his position I would have been saying good things about him, too. You see, you can't lose by loving.

Leading psychologists tell us there are two emotional needs inside every human being: to love and to be loved. Your relationship with your husband is one of the most important relationships in your entire span of years on this earth. Love him enough to make him your friend, your best friend. You will never be sorry you did.

6

For the Sake of
Your Children

Proverbs 31 talks about the "wife of noble character" who is "worth far more than rubies" (v. 1). Perhaps the most beautiful promise for any mother is found toward the end of this chapter: "Her children arise and call her blessed" (v. 28).

All Christian women would like to be known for the kind of noble character described in this passage. Yet so many of us struggle with poor self-image and the feeling that others don't respect or value us—especially our own children. Sadly, parents today often take the attitude that whether or not their children grow up to love and respect them or to live in a godly way is just a matter of chance. This is not true.

There is something we can do to insure that our children will call us blessed. We can live in a way that will make them say, "My mother was happy, blessed by God, a godly woman. I want the same kind of godly marriage she and Dad shared." What a blessing to think that we can have this kind of effect on our children! And the key to such an influence is to love the father of your children.

If you have been divorced from the father of your children, I'm not trying to put you off. Even a divorced woman can show respect for her former husband as a human being by refusing to belittle him or recite all his faults in front of his children. Many women do this because they fear their former husbands may be talking them down to the children, and they want to win the children to their side. But there will be time enough when the children are grown to give them a more mature view of what went wrong. And you can do more to win your children—not just to yourself, but also to a godly viewpoint—by always speaking words of respect for your former spouse. This will impress your children far more than name-calling or complaining.

For those who are struggling with the everyday rough spots of marriage, the same rule applies: If you want to make a godly impact on your children, love their father! You see, in child-rearing, we need to keep two simple and basic principles in mind.

First, a father probably has the greatest influence on his children's self-image. Christian counselors have learned that an individual's childhood view of his earthly father usually becomes his view of his heavenly Father. If a child is taught by his mother that Dad is to be respected, the child will grow to have an innate respect for God as well. If a mother plants rebellion, complaining and distrust in a child's heart, however, he is likely to struggle not only against his father, but against God, too. Obviously, this is not what we want for our children.

I painfully recall a Christian couple who had two

lovely daughters. For reasons unknown to me, the father drifted away from God and his family. He began to drink, got involved with another woman, and spent less and less time with his girls. Consequently, they developed a deep sense of being rejected.

As they grew and their father became untrustworthy, the girls manifested those negative feelings in their behavior—especially the older daughter. She quit attending church and fell deep into sin, searching for the male love that should have come from her dad. She also refused to trust or worship God, not realizing how her perception of Him had been tainted by her father's example.

Unfortunately, the last I heard of this young woman, she had shown up on a friend's doorstep. She was drunk and immodestly dressed, and she reported tearfully that she was planning to go live with her father, who had moved to another state. I can't overstate how important a father is to his children's self-image and perception of God.

Second, the childhood home is the primary training ground for marriage. Young people get their view of marriage, the roles they are to play in a later, adult relationship and what their homes will be like from the homes in which they grow up.

It's heartbreaking to think of the climbing divorce rate in America and other Western countries. By conservative estimates, *forty percent* of marriages in the U.S. end in divorce. And there is no way to tell the vast number of children who are growing up in what are known as dysfunctional homes—homes in which there are serious marital or emotional problems. All this heart-ache can do nothing but breed more pain and insecurity.

For years while Willard and I were in music ministry, we were repeatedly exposed to poor marriage relation-ships. In talking with those who came up for prayer or a word of counseling after we sang, we saw how their parents' bad marriages had hindered their job perfor-mance and their relationships with their spouses, children and the Lord. This was most visible during the visits we made to correctional facilities. We sang one song in particular that assured our listeners they were loved and special. Time and again, those hardened men or women would come up to us weeping, confessing that no one had ever told them they were special. They would usually spill out a story about having grown up in a home where their parents hated each other or fought constantly.

It's plain, then, that the destruction brought by a love-less marriage is echoed through the generations. So let's focus on positive, life-building things we can do to af-fect our children for the good.

Willard and I certainly didn't have a perfect marriage. But we loved each other very much. Because I had been brought up in a home where my mother loved and respected my dad, I knew this was the right thing to do—even when I felt hurt or neglected or did not agree with a certain decision. The benefits of that choice (I should say those many choices) have spilled over into the lives of others in surprising ways.

For instance, one of our sons had a young friend who spent a lot of time in our home while growing up. This person wrote me and said things after Willard's death that still bring tears to my eyes.

> Watching you in everyday situations has caused my view of marriage to be restored. As you know, I came from a broken home where my parents' marriage ended in divorce. For a long time, I felt that I didn't really want to be married because of all the hurt and bitterness I saw in marriage.
>
> Being around you caused me to see what God really intended marriage to be all about. In fact, it was through you that I found the strength and confidence to be able to commit myself to marriage.
>
> Your wonderful relationship was a miracle in my life, because Jesus used your love for each other as an example of a healthy, happy, loving, Christian marriage. I will be forever grateful for the healing effect the two of you together have had on my life.

Never underestimate the effects of a godly, loving marriage. How can you love your husband in such a way as to sow seeds of godliness, peace and joy in the lives of your children?

Support Their Father's Authority

The first thing I recommend is to have a loving respect for your husband and his place of authority in the home. Your respect will be an example to your children, helping them to grow up with respect for authority and for

God's laws and Word. This will make it easier for them to understand leadership and what it means to be a leader when their time comes to go into the world on their own.

It's vital to remember that a man is no more of a leader than he is with his own children. And we women either contribute to a respect for his leadership or undermine our husbands. How does this work?

One of the most common ways women undermine their husbands' authority is in the process of disciplining the children. A man has the God-given responsibility for the discipline and order of his household. He should set the disciplinary standards for the children. Because men are generally tough-minded when it comes to discipline and women tend to be more gentle, conferring brings a good balance. But as in all other areas, the man is to have the final authority.

The problem comes when you take sides with your children against a decision their dad has made. This often happens because you think a punishment is too strict or given out too quickly, without knowledge of all the circumstances, or simply because your husband was tired and irritable. These things may be true, but you should never take sides with your children against their father. Children can easily read our attitudes.

The problem can be compounded when your husband becomes aware that you're siding with the children and feels you're being disloyal to him. He may also feel that you're trying to win the children to yourself.

Willard and I learned a lot about this by observing other couples even before we had children. Often, we would see a father correct a child, only to have his wife openly or in a subtle way disagree with his correction. Sometimes, we saw women be strongly critical of their husbands' correction. This is confusing to a child. It says to him, "Your father is cruel and unjust. I love you more than he does." And when a woman lets a child think he can come to her if he doesn't agree with Dad's direction or authority, it can breed in that child a deceitful and manipulative spirit. Men know exactly what's going on when women do this, and it's little wonder they get angry!

I can't say I always agreed with Willard's correction of our sons. But two things helped me in this: First, I knew of his deep love for the boys, even though I sometimes thought he was too strict. Second, he was consistent. He didn't punish them in fits of anger, and when he promised a punishment, they got it. Third, when the boys were spanked—sometimes, I felt, too hard—it always amazed and blessed me to see them crawl up on their dad's lap for comfort when it was all over.

But when there was unfair discipline or spanking that I thought was too hard, I kept one rule in mind: When I confronted or appealed to Willard, it was *in private*. I never wanted to cause a split between Willard and the children or to undermine his authority with them. And because he knew I was protecting his position of authority, he was much more willing to consider my opinion.

The underlying principle is this: God intends child-rearing to bring husband and wife together, learning how to work with each other. Too often, parents let issues of child discipline pull them apart. But if you learn to work together, you and your children will be much better off for it.

Love Their Father Best

A second major way you can sow good seeds in the lives of your children is to place your love for your husband before your love for them. This sounds contradictory, but it's not.

This is another area in which relationships between husbands and wives break down. As soon as the first child comes along, many women feel torn, or they set their first love for their husbands aside. They think, After all, this baby is so tiny and helpless, and he's a grown man. He doesn't need me as much as this child. It's true that we go through seasons when the welfare of small children, especially infants, takes a major effort. But we don't have to neglect our children in order to place our love for our husbands in first place. I'm advocating a balance, of course.

It was hard for me to place my love for the children in proper perspective. Whenever Willard wanted to do something special just with me, I'd say, "We can take the children, too, can't we?" It was so hard for me to leave them when they were younger. Eventually, in response to my neglect of him in favor of the boys, Willard got in the habit of turning on the TV and falling asleep after dinner. I became defensive and spent even more time fussing with our sons.

It took an eye-opening experience—finding worn-out sheets in the linen closet, chipped china and a dented table top—to make me realize our marriage had lost its sparkle. And it took letting go of my motherly over-protectiveness of the boys to begin rebuilding our marriage relationship.

Demonstrating that you love and cherish your mate means spending time together. Taking time for each other is one thing many couples do not do, especially after they've been together for a while. When you take time to be together, you find that you automatically share dreams and hopes. A relationship works much easier when you're not trying to read each other's mind. When children are around, however, time together is difficult to find.

I recall the days when it seemed we couldn't carry on an adult conversation because every other sentence was interrupted. Usually, the interruption was a matter of life and death, of course. ("I can't find my Superman shirt!" "My baseball glove isn't on top of the car, where I left it!") The carefree days of young marriage were gone, but Willard and I determined that the romance didn't have to disappear.

After our get-away weekend in San Francisco, we decided we were going to demonstrate our oneness to our children. For example, it was just a small thing, but we decided we would no longer allow the children to sit between us. (It's amazing how often a small child will wiggle his way in between adults!) They could sit beside us, or sometimes on our laps, but never between us.

Because it was so hard to get time to talk alone, Willard and I had an extra-large bathtub built into our new home. We loved to bathe together, and we also found it to be about the only waking hour when we could talk without interruption. The bathroom door was locked, and unless there was a dire emergency, the boys knew they were not to bother us.

Now I'm not suggesting you have to take on our rules for your household, though you may want to. But if I get across nothing else in this book, I will stress this: Communicate with your man. Be creative. Make your solutions to problems fun. Keep refining your marriage and your home life until you find the things that work best for you.

Nevertheless, the basic principle holds: Put your love for your husband first. Don't allow your children to come between you and him in matters of discipline, in affection or in communication.

The Result: Secure Children

After Willard died, each of my sons told me the same thing in his own way: "One of the best things Dad left us was the blessing of knowing that he loved you, Mom." And now that they're more mature, they can see that of all the good things Willard did *with* them— hunting, fishing, sports—the most important thing he did *for* them was to give them security through our stable, loving relationship. I know this inner security gave the boys great strength when we went through the trauma of losing their father. They were a true support to me because they were secure in themselves.

Proverbs 31:28 says to me that it is well-adjusted, healthy, secure children who can give themselves to others. Children whose parents have bad marriages generally don't like to stick around the home. But when you have a good marriage, your love will be attractive, and it will draw your children back to your side, where they will bless you. And what a blessing that is!

Loving your husband is the first step in creating a home that is a spiritual and emotional shelter for the hearts of your children—a home where they can grow into the godly children you want them to be.

7

Loving for a Dark Tomorrow

It seems we often see things best only in contrast. Darkness makes light seem lighter and death makes life seem brighter. Loss makes us appreciate so much more the love we have today, flaws and all.

We are not promised any tomorrows, nor are we promised that all our tomorrows will be bright. To have only bright tomorrows would be wonderful. We live, however, in a real world. And when my dark tomorrow came, I prayed, "Does it have to be *so* dark, Lord?"

The first thing I did after Willard's death was to look back at all our beautiful memories. I remembered the love we shared as young newlyweds; the joy of bringing home our first tender-skinned newborn; the struggles and joys of building up our farming business; the years of sitting side-by-side with Willard in church. Pictures of the past flooded into my head.

These wonderful memories made me realize how important it is to live each day with someone as if it were our last. As never before, I saw the need to not "let the sun go down while you are still angry" (Eph. 4:26) and to live without regrets. Even in the days right after Willard's death, however, one thought kept crossing my mind: How long could I go on living on memories?

Later we'll look at some of the spiritual lessons you'll need to know to go on with your life when you have lost a loved one by death, divorce or separation, or even if you're a married woman forced to fend for yourself. But here I want to discuss some very practical things you need to know now in the event of a dark tomorrow.

Financial Matters

Some men feel they are doing their wives a favor by not involving them in financial, business or insurance matters. Many women feel this is a favor, too. In fact, some Christian women wrongly consider this being sheltered from the world by their husbands, who are their "spiritual covering." A husband is to be his wife's covering. But that means he is the one responsible in the final analysis for the family's spiritual, physical, emotional and financial well-being. He must set the tone and direction in these areas, but God did not mean for your husband to bear these burdens alone.

In Genesis 2:18, we read that God created Eve to be "a helper suitable for him." That means you are to be a helper who is fitted to your husband and capable of assisting him in all areas of life. To do that, ladies, we must be informed and involved in all his affairs insofar as it is possible.

Choosing to be involved has a lot of pluses as well as minuses. It takes much understanding and patience on the part of both husband and wife. You may have days when you ask, "Is it really worth it?" The answer is yes. For one thing, you will find great need to work at your communication, and whenever you do that, your love grows. You'll also have a greater understanding of the pressures on your husband. And, of course, it will make you better able to handle your business and financial matters alone in the event that it becomes necessary.

Shortly after Willard's death, I came across a special section in *Farm Wife News* on the subject of going on alone. It offered the following list of materials and information a woman should gather to prepare for the possibility of being on her own (reprinted with permission):

1. *Life insurance.* Where are the policies kept? List your policies by company, policy number, face amount, agent, premium due date and any loans against the policy.

2. *Safe deposit box.* What are the number and location? Where are the keys kept?

3. *Mortgages, leases and other periodic payments.* When are they due? List the amounts, names and addresses of those to whom these are payable and the repayment terms.

4. *Real estate holdings.* Where are the deeds or contracts kept? Itemize each, with the approximate value, price paid, any mortgage and the names of joint owners, if any.

5. *Other items to list:* bank accounts; titles of vehicles; installment payments (due dates and amounts); moneys owed to family and others; Social Security cards; old

income tax returns and canceled checks; account books or other business books; partnerships and other business agreements; stocks, futures or forward contracts held and the name of the broker; burial plots and arrangements; preferred guardian for your children; executor or trustee preferred; name and address of your lawyer; name and address of your accountant.

This list can be tailored to your individual situation and needs. Once all the materials are gathered, make several copies of everything. Put one in a safe deposit box or other secure place. This could save hours of searching and worry at a time when you don't need the added pressure of wondering if your affairs are in order.

Funeral Arrangements

People often have a hard time discussing their spouse's wishes in the event of death. Christians can take the attitude, "I don't want to think about death, because I've got the life of Christ in me. My spirit is going on to live with Jesus, so what do I care what they do with my physical body?" I don't mean to be disrespectful about such a private subject, but when you die, somebody will be left to do something with your body! It is an act of love and wisdom to discuss these matters in advance.

If you love your husband, you will become his "suitable helper" today. He will then have the comfort of knowing you will be able to function well in the event of a dark tomorrow.

Separation

Even if you don't lose your spouse to a premature death, I am well aware that many women face another kind of dark tomorrow. They can suffer the same kind of grief when their marriages break up. Unfortunately, Christian couples are not exempt from these pressures.

When problems arise in a marriage, too many Christian women these days are tempted to think, Why not just get a divorce? After all, we're under grace, aren't we? If you're in a difficult position and are thinking these thoughts, I want to encourage you that divorce is not the answer that non-Christians and the media make it out to be. I don't feel capable of addressing the theological issues surrounding divorce. Besides, others have already done that. But I do want you to consider some of the far-reaching, emotional ramifications of divorce.

Right after Willard's death (and probably because I was going through a grieving process), I became especially aware of people who were separated or divorced. I could sense in them the same kind of deep loneliness I was experiencing. And there were other feelings, too. They were struggling with the sense of rejection. They had been rejected by their spouses, so they were pulling away into a shell, isolating themselves from their friends and their brothers and sisters in Christ.

You cannot allow grief, whether because of death or divorce, to separate you from those who can give love and support. True, times of quiet and being alone are necessary to work through grief. But more than that, you need the affirmation of friends. You need to be exposed to the common, ongoing aspects of life, for life does go on, whether you want it to at the moment or not!

Second, for those who want a divorce, consider that divorce is not the end of a relationship, especially when there are children involved. Again, others have written about the long-lasting, emotional impact of divorce. I want to speak to you about the practical effects.

When a married couple with children decide to divorce, they never lose their connectedness because of the children. At the time of the divorce, the wife may think, Well, we'll file for joint custody—I'll have them during the week, and he can see them every other weekend. But the decisions and struggles of child-rearing don't end there. It's not as simple as a one-time decision. Raising children requires many decisions and lots of dialogue concerning holidays, vacations and so on. If your inability to communicate or love your husband is a major obstacle, how much more struggle will you have when you need to communicate about delicate and important issues that involve your children?

Some dear friends of ours saw their marriage end in divorce. Afterward, the usual discussions about such things as where their sons would spend Christmas were complicated by the fact that the father moved to another state. Later, when the boys reached high school age, they said they wanted to live with Dad rather than Mom because he was more permissive. Naturally, a whole new round of talks followed. And when the sons were ready to marry, their divided loyalties created the need for still another level of diplomacy.

Truly, children tie a father and mother together for life.

Knowing the open attitude about divorce today, I write these things with real caution. I also pray that God's wisdom and love will come through my words, because the last thing I want to do is point the finger at someone who is in a difficult marriage or who has already gone through divorce. I believe divorce is a sin, but it's a sin like any other and can be dealt with by turning your heart to God.

For those of you going through a dark tomorrow today, I want to affirm, one more time, that you just cannot lose by loving. Even in a situation that ends in a way you don't want, or when it seems your prayers weren't answered, you are not the loser if you love until the end.

To all wives, I want to say: Love with all your heart today. Then no matter what tomorrow brings, joy and oneness or the sorrow of separation, you will have lived a rich life, and its inner rewards will go on and on.

8

Going On

L ike the previous chapter, this one is written to women who have lost their husbands. Your loss may have come through death or divorce. Or perhaps you have lost your husband emotionally. It may seem that, like the prodigal son, he is in a far country, and you're waiting, hoping he will come home to your heart.

At once, you may be saying, I don't want to go on living without a loving husband at my side—I don't think I'm strong enough to do it. I can honestly say I know exactly how you feel. When Willard went to be with the Lord, my wonderful world fell apart. Not long after, a friend came to tell me that other friends were asking, "What is poor LeeAnn going to do now without Willard?"

"What did you tell them?" I asked.

"I told them you're tough," my friend said, smiling. "I told them you'll make it."

The truth was that I didn't feel tough at all. Many days, I sat there on the sofa, feeling devastated, not knowing which way to turn or what to do next. I didn't want to go on. This may be hard for some to understand, but I was brokenhearted and didn't even want to go on living. Being on my own made me feel unfulfilled and empty. What's more, there seemed to be no one to whom I could reveal my true feelings.

Keeping a Journal

So I began to do something that helped me get a handle on all the rampaging emotions I felt. It's something simple that any woman can do to minister to herself in hard times: Keep a journal.

Right after Willard's death, friends kept coming to tell me what Willard meant to them. Some told me how much our love for each other and our solid marriage meant to them. I can remember thinking, through the numbness, I'll have to write all these good things down so I can recall them later. Maybe it will be helpful for the boys. A close friend prompted me to write these stories down as well. She seemed to feel an urgency about capturing on paper the things I had learned about the love of a woman for her husband. Somewhere inside of me, I felt this prompting, too. But to be honest, I did nothing about it at first.

Eventually, another close friend heard about my desire to have a record of my years with Willard and gave me a little blank book to write in. The first friend I mentioned had done some of the writing down of stories for me, so I transferred these things into my own book. I recorded events that were funny and touching and many that were very personal. I called this book my "Bear It Book," because when I was hurting, I could open it up and be truly helped to bear the pain. Just rereading my entries became a source of strength.

One of my warm entries concerned a little neighbor boy named Reed. He loved Willard so much and enjoyed teasing with him. And Reed's mom told me that a night or two after Willard's death, as she was tucking him in bed, Reed asked, "What do you think is going on in heaven? Do you think there are tractors up there?"

She thought for a moment, then replied, "Well, Reed, heaven is a happy place, so if you want a tractor there, there will probably be tractors."

Reed said, "What kind of tractors do you think they have there?"

"I suppose they have whatever kind you want—Ford, John Deere or whatever."

"I guess that takes care of that," Reed said. "Willard's driving a Ford."

The next night at bedtime, Reed said, "Mom, what do you think is going on in heaven tonight? Do you suppose they have tractor pulls?"

His mother smiled, now knowing what her five-year-old was thinking. He had seen Willard participate in a tractor pull shortly before his death, and Willard's Ford had outpulled Reed's dad's John Deere. She remembered all the fun Willard had shared with Reed after that victory, showing him the trophy and joking about the contest. So she said, "I suppose they just might have tractor pulls if that's what you want."

"Brother," Reed said, "that means I'm going to have to look at all those dumb trophies Willard wins before I get there."

After recording this story in my journal, I wrote,

"Jesus is so good. He knew I needed to hear this sweet child's thoughts. Even the children loved Willard. Who didn't?"

Dwelling on the good things life has given us makes the dark, discouraging days so much more bearable. As the apostle Paul said, "Whatever is true...noble...right...pure...lovely...admirable—if anything is excellent or praiseworthy—think about such things" (Phil. 4:8).

My "Bear It Book" was truly a joy. But some months after I began it, yet another friend came to me and said, "LeeAnn, your book is such a good idea, and I know it's very helpful for you. But don't you have any bad feelings, too? You can't just keep them all bottled up inside. So what are you going to do with them?" I admitted to her that there were many feelings I'd been suppressing—thoughts like, Why am I alone now? and prayers like, "God, why weren't You there to save Willard's life when I needed You?"

You may laugh, but a short time later, another lady went out and bought me another little blank book! This one I called my "Ugly Book." On its pages, I recorded all the bad feelings I was experiencing. I kept track of the questioning prayers I prayed, as well as the Scripture verses or other answers that came into my head in response to those why kinds of prayers (for example, 1 Thess. 4:13-18; Ps. 56:8; Heb. 13:5).

My "Ugly Book" also became a source of strength. First, it gave me an outlet for my feelings when I was too upset to let them show to other people. Second, it gave me a record to look at when I heard myself praying those why prayers again and again. Then I could see God's replies to my questions and feel His comfort all over again.

One of the principles I learned from this simple act of keeping a journal was that, when God prompts you to do something, go ahead and *do it*. I found that obeying these small promptings opened the way to greater things I could not have imagined. More about that in a moment.

Opening Up

Writing became one source of comfort for me, a way of ministering to my own soul. But there's a second kind of ministry I had to become open to, the ministry of others. This was more difficult than I could have imagined.

I've already mentioned the friends who were around me. Yet I felt a great distance from them at first. I hurt so much inside that, like a wounded animal, I didn't want anyone to get close enough to touch that pain. Many of us also have an inbred kind of pride, and it comes as an inner voice that says, Come on. Be strong. This is what everyone expects from you. You can't ask people to put up with your tears. Put on a smile, and be brave.

The apostle Paul wrote, however, "Carry each other's burdens, and in this way you will fulfill the law of Christ" (Gal. 6:2). How can others minister to us if we are prideful and unwilling to open up and reveal our feelings?

Eventually, I found that I had to let others inside to see the real me—the me who wasn't strong, who didn't

have all the Christian answers ready at hand, who sometimes got mad at God or did not understand in the least
why my husband had died. It was in allowing others
to handle this pain with me that much more healing
came.

I recall how one friend phoned me from a city halfway
across the country, "LeeAnn," she said, "I am calling
to say that I don't know what to say." How her honesty
and vulnerability touched me. Other friends affected me
in similar ways. Cards, phone calls, visits: all these
small acts of caring added up to a shower of love. When
others reached out to me, it became easier to share the
lonely times. When the hurt was more than I could bear
any longer, it seemed that someone would phone or drop
by. I came to see these "coincidences" as God's way
of nudging people who would help me bear my burden.

Trusting God

The apostle Paul encouraged us, saying, "Cast all
your anxiety on [God] because he cares for you" (1 Pet.
5:7). It isn't so hard, really, to cast your cares upon
the Lord. What's hard is leaving them there! So often
we feel that God is not working fast enough to heal our
hurts or to answer our prayers. We become impatient.
It is so hard to relax in Him and trust, isn't it?

When all is going well, it's easy to say, "Of course
I trust God" or "If you've got a problem, just trust God
and He'll help you." These things come off the tongue
so readily when we can see the road ahead. But the
moment change is thrown at us and we're wandering
blindly, there goes our trust. It need not be that way,

however. In fact, when we're willing to launch out into God's care during these dark times, He is able to do something new and altogether wonderful with our lives.

Sometimes I like to try to turn the picture around by imagining what God feels like when we're slow to trust or we refuse to hear and obey Him. Imagine the frustration from His point of view! Like a loving Father, He wants to fulfill our deepest needs—if only we will let go of our fear and take His hand. Then He'll lead us.

The third and most important ministry you need to help you recover from the devastation of loss is the ministry God Himself wants to perform in your life. After all, He is the one best able to reach into the deepest places of your soul and bring the healing touch, isn't He?

In some ways, after Willard's death, I had to learn about trusting God all over again. I'd said for a long time that I trusted God, but that was when I had a husband to provide for me and give me love. Now that I had this terrifying sense of being on my own again, I wondered about God: Does He really know my needs? Can I trust Him to do the best thing for my life? My mind could say yes, but my heart was hesitant to answer. I tell the following brief story in answer to these questions, knowing some of you are asking, too.

A number of friends had suggested I develop my "Bear It Book" into a larger manuscript that might be of help to other women. As one friend put it, "The Bible says that the older women ought to teach the younger women how to love their husbands." That made me one of the older women! I didn't think I was ready for that. Besides—write a book? I've never even been good at spelling. I pushed the idea out of my mind.

In the meantime, my son Mark and his wife, Laurie, decided to become involved with an international organization called Youth With a Mission. We'd known about this excellent ministry for some time and were happy with the work they were doing, training and sending missionaries to nations all around the world. I thought it was a good idea for Mark and Laurie to try a short-term venture through YWAM. And after they became involved, I decided to take part in a special YWAM school for folks in their middle years. This school, appropriately known as a Crossroads Discipleship Training School, was to alter my life.

During one of the morning sessions, a man named Dan Snead, from California, was talking to us about learning to hear God's voice. (Knowing you can hear God's voice is, of course, a necessary step in learning to trust Him.) I had heard that this man was blessed with a special gift of insight from God.

You must understand that I'm the conservative type. I believe that when God speaks to you through another person it will be to confirm something He has already communicated to you in your heart. So I felt quite reserved when, at the end of the session, Dan Snead said he was going to demonstrate how God can communicate to us through special gifts He gives to others in the body of Christ. Yet I couldn't escape the feeling I'd had on my way to the school that God was going to give me some special direction for my life there.

The session was to end at noon, and of the eighty-seven people in the class, Dan had spoken to many, but not to me. Was I relieved or disappointed? I couldn't tell. But just when I thought he was going to end the session, Dan looked at me. He pointed me out and asked my name, which I told him.

"LeeAnn," he said, "you sing, don't you?" Though I was speechless, my roommate quickly confirmed this. "In fact," Dan went on, "the Lord has confirmed to me that you were involved in a singing ministry for a long time—a family group."

My mind raced, thinking about our eighteen years with the Good Shepherd Quartet and Families. How could this stranger know these things unless the Lord were revealing them to him? He certainly had my attention.

"This group was your identity, but you were not completely fulfilled in it."

"Please, God," I prayed silently, "don't tell him everything!" Only Willard had known that the singing ministry was not completely fulfilling for me. Oh, and of course God also knew.

"The ministry was fulfilling to you because of your family," Dan said, smiling. "But God wants you to have your own identity now and fulfillment in your own ministry."

A ministry? What on earth?

"The Lord is showing me that you have had a very bad hurt in your life. You've come through a dark time." Then he looked directly at me and asked, "Have you ever thought of writing a book?"

When that session closed, I couldn't dodge God's direction any longer. I had to trust that He was leading me into new directions, including something that seemed ridiculous to me: writing.

The main point I want to make from this story is this: When unsettling times come, you can trust God to lead you. In fact, after suffering a devastating loss, your life can only become rich and rewarding again when you cast your cares upon God and trust Him to direct you. This means letting go of your fear, which really comes from a desire to control your life yourself.

Tell God you want to trust Him; you want Him to take charge of your life. Ask Him to take charge of your husband if you are emotionally or physically apart. If you're divorced or your husband has passed on, ask God to take charge of your loneliness. Give Him all that is in your life, and ask Him to make it over new. If you sense that inside you are really unwilling for this, ask Him to help you become willing.

But above all, don't sit and wait for the feeling of willingness to come over you, as if God has to let you know He's there by tickling your rib cage. Ask Him to guide you gently in the first steps you are to take in building your new life in Him. Finding God's plan for your life may not be easy at first when your head is clouded with loss. I know it wasn't easy for me. I so longed to have a deeper relationship with someone, to love and be loved. This thought seemed to occupy most of my waking moments.

In prayer one day, however, I realized God was speaking in the stillness of my heart. I heard the words, "Not until you are satisfied and fulfilled and content with being loved by Me alone!" I felt a stab of pain—

and then a rush of joy. Yes, I would choose to trust Him to love me, no matter what came.

Before you try to run out and plan a new life for yourself, I caution you: Stop planning! Stop wishing! Allow Him to give you the most thrilling plan for your life, one you cannot even imagine. Be patient and wait, for He wants the very best for you. Look to Him every morning for what He wants to do in your life that day. You'll find He leads you one day, one step, at a time. I've learned that when I live like this, simply, He will give me the perfect peace He promised to all those who would follow Him (see John 14). And one morning, He will wake you to surprises beyond your wildest dreams.

Let me tell you now what He did for me.

9

God's Plans for You

From the outset, my purpose in this book has been to offer biblical principles that will help you fulfill an important part of God's will for you: to love your husband. I want to tell you now what God did for me and in me after Willard's death, how He worked out His plans for me, even through dark and dismal times. I hope it encourages you, for it illustrates a vital, scriptural principle every woman needs to know about God's will regarding her marriage and her husband.

Willard had been gone a little more than two years. It was summer, time for the harvest. I'd always loved harvest, but now it had lost its joy for me. It only made me lonely for my husband.

In many ways, life was limping along. I'd had the brief discipleship training through YWAM, and I was scheduled to go on a short-term missionary venture in Asia in the fall. Mark and Laurie had been with YWAM for some months. In fact, Mark had had his own remarkable experiences with healing after the death of his dad.

While on the mission field, Mark had met another young man named Matt Rawlins, who was teaching for

YWAM. Matt's mother was dying of cancer. Even the crackling phone connection that carried Mark's overseas call to me could not conceal the peace and joy Mark had found after this young man had prayed and discussed the Scriptures with him.

How I wished I felt that joy! The missions plans I'd made, good as they were, only filled up my waking hours. On one hand, I wanted to go to Asia. On the other hand, it was busyness, meant in part to help me avoid the empty hours that stretched before me, especially the nights—they were so long!

Occasionally, I would pull out a list I'd made some time after Willard's death and reread it. It was a list of all the qualities I wanted in a man if I ever remarried. Each time I reread the list, I suspected it would never happen. My qualifications seemed too specific, too lofty and demanding. The list went like this:

• He must be a man of God and not a new Christian. A spiritual leader.

• He must love my boys and have their approval.

• I'd like him to be handsome and fun-loving and have a good sense of humor.

• I'd like him to be involved in missions. (This one troubled me a little; Willard had left me well-off financially, and I didn't want to use this money to support someone. A financially independent man, then—with a heart for missions? Maybe I was stretching it a little.)

• I'd like him to love traveling.

• It would probably be best if he had lost his mate, too. We would probably understand each other better if we both knew about this kind of hurt.

Each time I reviewed the list, I had a sinking feeling. Surely there was no one anywhere who could fill this bill. I didn't want to make a mistake if I ever remarried, but maybe I'd given God too tall an order. Much of the time, I didn't think about my life or about remarrying at all. The hurt was too fresh. Maybe I'd remarry in three or four years—maybe longer. Most of my emotional energy went into making it from sunup to sundown.

Later in that "summer of the lonely harvest," some friends asked if I would be available to help with a YWAM training school at one of the mission's many bases, this one just forty miles from my home in Oregon. Knowing how I love to cook, they asked if I would help prepare meals. At first I hesitated. Then, knowing my son and our loyal employees could take care of the business, I decided it would do me good to get away again. That weekend, I made the drive.

Could This Be the One?

The man teaching on Monday morning was Duane Rawlins. Between rounds in the kitchen, I sat in on his classes. I quickly made some connections: Duane's son Matt was the young man who had lost his mom to cancer and had comforted my son Mark in his loss. It was nice to meet the father of such a godly young man. And I made some other, unexpected connections, too.

Duane Rawlins was a real man of God, a spiritual leader who knew the Scriptures and was an excellent teacher. I learned that he owned several successful businesses, which allowed him the freedom to travel widely, teaching mostly for YWAM. He was also good-looking and athletic. When I heard him speak about the death of his wife, Betty, and how much it had affected him, I knew he was a sensitive man who felt pain deeply.

I was getting nervous.

That noon, our mutual friends introduced us. (I believe you're right to think they had something in mind!) God took it from there.

Duane and I spent a lot of time together over the next few months. It didn't take us long to realize that it was God's desire for us to spend the rest of our lives together. Duane was everything on my list and more. When I told him that, he sheepishly pulled out his own list, one he'd written after Betty's death. That gave us both a good chuckle!

To make a long story short, we were married that Thanksgiving. The wedding was on a beach in Hawaii so that our children involved in missions in Asia and the others on the West Coast could come. The marriage gave me three more exceptional children, Mark, Mindy and Matt, plus their spouses, and it gave Duane and me a total of five grandchildren. My cup, which seemed so empty only months before, was full to overflowing.

Growing a Second Marriage

For some of you reading this book, this story may seem like a pretty fairy tale. But every word of it is true. It's also true that Duane and I have learned some basic lessons about love in a second marriage. Perhaps these lessons, which I'll explain briefly, will help others of you who are also entering or living in a second marriage.

First, a second marriage can become a time of starting over in your spiritual growth. Whether your first marriage ended by death or divorce, you are probably "a little older and a little wiser" regarding the important things of life. It seems that it takes loss and some hurt to teach us, doesn't it?

One of life's priorities that I had always put aside during my years with Willard was to stay consistently in God's Word. As a Christian, I knew this was vital. Even when we were involved in the music ministry, though, I always thought of consistent Bible reading and study as an obligation. Secretly, I might even have felt it was a little like drudgery, though I'd never have said it that way. In any case, I did not consider it a joy. So I did what most of us do when we want to avoid something that's good for us. I allowed busy details to crowd out time I could have spent with the Lord in His Word.

When Duane and I married, though, I sensed a need to renew my spiritual life. I really wanted to grow. I'd known Bible reading was important, but I needed help in consistency.

Now, together, Duane and I are committed to staying daily in God's Word. And I know my newfound consistency has come mostly from Duane's devotion to Bible study. We have entered into a kind of pact to study His Word, helping each other to reach for new spiritual goals.

Another lesson I learned is that it's possible to find a deeper intimacy in a second marriage, perhaps, than in your first.

For me, this came as I learned to be more free with my feelings when I talked to Duane—even my residual feelings of pain when I'm reminded of Willard. Like-wise, Duane says he has found freedom to share his lingering sorrow at thoughts of Betty's painful death, as well as wonderful memories that are so much a part of him.

In some second marriages, spouses don't allow each other to talk about previous husbands or wives, especially if there is anything good to say. Sometimes even stepchildren are not allowed to talk about the absent parent. We believe this is destructive. It's unrealistic to expect that someone your spouse once loved deeply should simply vanish from his emotional landscape, never to be mentioned again. Talking about your previous spouse, both the good and the bad, can promote intimacy and bring comfort and assurance. It may be one of the healthiest things you can do for each other.

Third, God has shown me that I can still be flexible enough to change. I'd like to tell you that in the years Duane and I have been married, I've never had to make any adjustments to him. But I expect you wouldn't believe that.

Willard, as I've said before, was not very expressive with words. For twenty-four years, I was used to living with a man who would express his appreciation with a nod or a pat, and maybe a kiss. So I assumed that, unless Willard said he didn't like something I was doing (and it took quite a bit to get a rise out of him), I was OK. When I married Duane, a gifted communicator, I was in for a big adjustment.

I took pride in my cooking. Of course a major flop was needed before Willard would scratch his chin and look at me questioningly. But those were few and far between—only a dry, tough pot roast here, a too-salty soup there. Not long after Duane and I married, however, I served up one of my breakfast favorites from my never-miss recipe for waffles. Duane almost always complimented my meals, so I was expecting some favorable comment as I sat down and picked up my fork.

Duane took a bite, then said casually, "These waffles are a bit soggy."

I was crushed. They *were* soggy just a little, but Willard would never have said a word! It took a few minutes of silent reflection before I composed myself to see what was happening. I'd already promised myself I wouldn't compare Duane to Willard, but God wanted to teach me something more. I saw how set in my ways I'd become, how I expected things to be the same.

I determined that morning that I would be flexible. Things would never be as they were when I was married to Willard. I would allow God to bring into my life, along with a new husband, new opportunities for me to grow in even the smallest of ways. I determined to make life with a second husband an adventure in growth, and that is what it has been.

God's Good Plans

I have related a few more events from my life only to illustrate a larger truth that you, too, can live by. It doesn't matter whether your husband has passed away, has physically or emotionally abandoned you, or whether you are simply struggling with some rough spots in your relationship. I want you to hang onto a

true word of encouragement; remember it every morning and throughout the day as you pray for your husband and your relationship. It is this:

> God will fulfill your dream of a wonderful
> marriage—and fulfill it beyond your wildest
> dreams—if only you will trust Him.

I can say this, not just because things worked out for
me after my heartbreak, but also on the authority of
Scripture. Listen to this wonderful promise from God
our Father: " 'I know the plans I have for you,' declares
the Lord, 'plans to prosper you and not to harm you,
plans to give you hope and a future' " (Jer. 29:11, emphasis added).

It could be that you have never prayed and given your
husband and your marriage relationship into God's
hands. Or perhaps you made that commitment on your
wedding day and since then you've been fretting and
trying to manage things your own way. I invite you now
to bow your head and pray. Tell God you believe His
promise for your marriage. Make Him the Lord of your
marriage. Give Him every little pocket of hurt or disappointment regarding your husband, and ask Him to fill
it up with His forgiveness. Ask Him to make your
marriage over—make it new!

You will never be sorry when you make this prayer-
ful commitment before God. He always keeps His
promises. You will also be amazed at the changes He
brings in your own heart and the new kind of love you
find there. And, as I've said before, you can't lose by
loving. Try it and see.

10

Loving in Life's Changing Seasons

A mother sent her older son out to pick berries in a wild patch of woods. The boy took nothing to carry the berries in. You can imagine their condition when he got back home and emptied them on the table—out of his pockets!

His mother said, ''Where is your common sense? The next time I send you to get something for me, have the presence of mind to carry it home in a box.''

Two days later, she sent him off to find his four-year-old brother who was playing at the home of a friend.

I'm sure you've already guessed the punch line. The older brother returns home with his little brother—kicking and screaming inside a big, cardboard box.

Sometimes we all need to be reminded that the methods that worked yesterday may not help us out to-day or tomorrow. Life changes. Circumstances change. People change.

One of the greatest mistakes we can make as wives is to be inflexible and resist change. You will be doing yourself a big favor if you'll remember that even your relationship with your husband is ever changing.

Perhaps you're thinking, Oh, no! My love for him will never change—I'll always love him just the way I do today. Or perhaps that news makes you happy. Maybe you've been going through a trying period in your marriage and you can't see even a hint of light in the darkness.

Let me assure you, every marriage goes through its changes and seasons. You may have a constant and good relationship and never go through a rough spell. But your emotional needs and your ability to give to one another will shift. Or, as I suggested, you may be thinking that things will never get better between you.

In either case, I want to help you see some of the changes that may yet lie ahead for you. I also want to help you understand how to love your husband best during these different seasons of life. We don't have to be like the boy in the story; we can be prepared to change the way we love in response to changing needs and circumstances.

The Newlywed Season

The first season you'll encounter is the period when you and your husband are newlyweds. By this I don't mean the very beginning of your married life, those first two or three years. I mean the time when you wake up in bed one morning, roll over, look at the guy next to you (the one snoring loud enough to make the neighbor's dog bark) and think with an edge of panic, I'm married to this man!

Once the rose-pink blush of early bliss fades into the mundane grays and browns of everyday life, you begin to realize that you are really and truly married. That is, you are wed *for life*—not to a dreamy Prince Charming who meets all your emotional, physical and financial needs, but to a guy who sometimes wants to fish all by himself or who asks you to move away from the TV so he doesn't miss the next kickoff. This is a rude awakening for many women as it was for me.

You can respond to this in a way that will help your love remain strong. Of course, you can apply this in every season of marriage, but the earlier you learn to do it, the better off you'll be.

Look for the good in your husband and your circumstances. The apostle Paul put it this way: ''Whatever is admirable—if anything is excellent or praiseworthy—think about such things'' (Phil. 4:8). Because we're human, and because we enter marriage with such high expectations, we too often focus on the negative. This is a fleshly, un-Christian reaction that we can learn to turn around.

Let's say you always wanted to marry a man who could support you and your children. Perhaps the guy you married was low man on the ladder of a small company, but you could see that he had a lot of potential. You hoped that before long you could quit your job and stay at home to raise the children or pursue other personal interests.

After five years of marriage, however, you woke up to the fact that other men in your husband's company are climbing the ladder, but he seems satisfied with his lower position. One day, you ask him why he isn't getting the raises and promotions.

"I like what I do," he says with a shrug. "I'm not one of these guys who wants to claw his way to the top. You have to do a lot of things you don't believe in if you want a key to the executive suite. That's not for me. Most of those guys have high blood pressure."

You may find yourself facing this or a similar situation. Whatever you've just awakened to, you now know you are married to a man who will probably never fully meet some inner hope or dream.

First, sit down with pen and paper and list all the good things about your husband. Focus on all that is praiseworthy, or the things you find negative will grow like weeds and choke out your love.

Second, burn all your bridges to the past. Stop comparing your husband to the other men you might have married. And stop measuring him against all the dreams you have held since you were a little girl. Face yourself in the mirror and say, "He will never be all that I hoped, and that's OK. I will love him as he is, because that is what I promised in my wedding vows." Even if he criticizes your cooking!

Waking up to disappointment is waking up to who *you* are. It's realizing the limits of your love. It's finding out how small and petty human love is. In the end, we all demand to have what we want. And that's a good point to come to, for when we see how self-centered we are, we can ask God to fill our unloving and inflexible hearts with His love. Only when you have reached this point have you found a solid platform on which to build.

God's love is the foundation that will make any

marriage steadfast and strong—if only we will ask Him for that love. And when we ask, He gives His love freely, in abundant measure (see Luke 6:38).

The Child-Rearing Season

Another season of marriage is the season of child-rearing. Adding children to a marriage throws some big challenges at you.

One of the first is the tendency a woman has to put her children before her husband. It's easy to slip into this. Children are so needy when they're small, and so demanding always. One day, it seems, you and your husband are enjoying quiet walks together along forested paths, or candlelit dinners for two. And then it hits. A child enters the picture and wrings every last ounce of love, patience and energy out of you.

If you're in the early stages of child-rearing, I must encourage you that it gets easier. You may not believe it now, but there will soon come a time when you are not on call twenty-four hours a day.

No matter how old your children are, I also want to encourage you to save something of yourself to give to your husband. There is no law saying that in order to be a good Christian mother you must give yourself so totally to your children that you feel like a wrung-out dishrag at the end of the day. (There will be enough days when you feel like that anyway!) Most husbands need just a little attention from someone who will stop long enough to give them a squeeze and a wink and say, "I love you, and I'm glad you're home."

Here are some simple ways you can love your

husband during those seemingly endless years of child-rearing:

• A man needs to know he is a good provider. Give him the gift of a few words of gratitude.

• A man needs to know his thoughts and values are important. Give him the gift of a few minutes of un-divided attention. Ask his opinion, and tell him why it's helpful to you.

• A man needs to know you and his children respect him. Give him the gift of a few words of praise. When your children are present, mention one of his traits that you admire.

• A man needs to know he is desired. It's not too much to ask that you get the kids to bed early or ship them off to Grandma's once in a while—and then slip into something comfortable.

• A man needs to know he can be himself, even when he comes up short. Give him the gift of confidence and confidentiality. It takes only a moment to say, "I forgive you, and I love you no matter what."

• A man needs a woman who is strong, who is grow-ing toward godly maturity. Give him the gift of spend-ing time with God each day so you are becoming more like Christ. Find your fulfillment not in a career or children or even in your husband; find it by growing in the Lord.

Perhaps the most important thing to learn during the busy, demanding season of child-rearing is this: Sow small acts and words of love patiently, constantly, the way a farmer plants seeds, and you will reap a continual harvest of love from your man.

I remember some precious times when the boys were small and I'd bundle them up so we could all go with Willard in the truck while he ran some errand. It was a little thing, but it showed him I wanted to be with him even sometimes when it was inconvenient. And such little things add up.

The Mid-life Season

A third season in your love for your husband comes in mid-life. In fact, for your husband, this may be the time when he most needs your love.

Today, we hear a lot about men who reach mid-life—that is, their forties or fifties—only to hit an emotional crisis. Popularly, it's called a mid-life crisis, and it's characterized by a man's loss of confidence, mourning of missed opportunities, restlessness, a sudden change of behavior. But even if mid-life is not a time of major upheaval for your husband, it will most likely be a time when he reassesses his life. He may seem to be pulling away from you. It will almost certainly be a time when he needs your love in a new and different way.

If your husband has reached mid-life and his boat seems to be rocking a little, your love can be a steadying influence. Naturally, by mid-life you will have gotten used to your husband's habits and mannerisms. If you sense a sudden change, especially restlessness, your first response may be panic. You may think, He's dissatisfied with me.

At this point, you may try desperately to assure yourself of his love by forcing yourself into his arms and his most private thoughts. But your efforts will only be an attempt to hear words you want to hear, to be assured that nothing has changed. You may feel as if your emotional boat is rocking, too, and that you are trying to steady things for yourself and not for him at all.

The best way to love your husband in this season of mid-life reassessment is to remember that he needs you to be stable. I'm not suggesting this is easy, because any changes he makes also affect you. But if you focus only on yourself and not on his needs, you'll never have the chance to help him through a rough period.

Second, you can remind your husband of all he has accomplished in his life so far. It's common for men in mid-life—even men who once seemed contented—to be seized with an overwhelming remorse. They may think of all the career opportunities they could have taken, of the things they could have done with their children. They may even relive long-past mistakes they "should" never have made.

It's important that you don't make his lost dreams or missed opportunities seem trivial. Don't say, "Oh, it doesn't matter that you're not chairman of the board." To him, at that moment, it matters. You must gently, consistently remind him of all he has accomplished. This will be a lot easier if you've spent time focusing on his good points. The fact that you value his life and accomplishments will help him regain perspective.

You may also feel threatened and sense that a major change is coming. Your husband suddenly starts talking about moving to a distant city, joining the foreign legion or quitting his high-paying job to open a surf shop in the Bahamas. In his desperation to find himself, he may even hint that you separate.

Whether or not he suggests uprooting your comfortable life to do something drastic or crazy, let him know you're with him all the way. Tell him, in the words of Ruth,

> Don't urge me to leave you or to turn back from you. Where you go I will go, and where you stay I will stay. Your people will be my people and your God my God. Where you die I will die, and there I will be buried. May the Lord deal with me, be it ever so severely, if anything but death separates you and me (Ruth 1:16-17).

So many of us wrote those words into our wedding ceremonies. We stood and gazed into the eyes of our young bridegrooms and vowed them with all our hearts. Now, in mid-life, we need to take stock of promises made in our youth. And we need to renew our courage to live by them.

A friend once described a mid-life crisis he and his wife went through and how they handled it. As the years went by after their marriage, he became more and more involved in his work, often being away from home on business for several days at a time. She became more and more wrapped up in their children. Gradually a deadening of feelings occurred in both of them. The red tape of duty took over their relationship, and the intimacy disappeared.

Then one day, on a business trip plane ride, the husband met a young woman whose husband had recently left her for another woman. Because of his love for people and skills in counseling, our friend talked with her. The next day, he called to see how she was doing and spent an hour on the phone with her. Perhaps because of the safety of being on the phone or his own deep need for affection, he began to discuss his own feelings, and consequently he experienced a warmth he had been missing for several years.

All at once, he was overwhelmed and frightened by thoughts about this woman that he found going through his head. He told me later that he was so grateful he had been in a telephone booth and not the woman's house at that point.

Being a Christian who was still deeply committed to his wife in spite of the coldness of their relationship, he chose to go home and tell her about the whole experience. And she proved to be a wise and loving mate, listening empathetically rather than critically, admitting her own vulnerability. As a result, what could have been a disaster instead became a means of drawing them together and renewing their determination to keep their marriage fresh and exciting.

The Senior Season

The other season most of us will face with our husbands is the senior years. As I am just approaching this season in my own life, I write from my observations of other marriages.

This senior season can be a gentle and yet stimulating time as your love moves into another phase. At this time, you will be called upon to love your husband in the face of both new challenges and promises.

One challenge a man may face is the feeling that he has outlived his usefulness. A man's identity is so bound up with what he does and accomplishes (as opposed to what kind of person he is) that most men feel they are being forced to retire—that they're being put out to pasture.

These men respond by becoming restless and irritable. They don't want to sit still and do nothing. They hate the idea of retiring to Florida to play shuffleboard and golf every day. Some wives simply make themselves scarce, or they warn the grandchildren to stay away because "Grandpa is in one of his cranky moods."

On the other hand, it may be that your husband eagerly volunteers to take an early retirement. His calendar is filled with plans for fishing ventures and cross-country trips. Yet many of these men quickly find the free life of retirement boring and empty. This is the time when a wife can gently walk alongside her husband, pointing out the other kinds of productive things he can do. I am talking about things that will continue to build Christlikeness in him.

Primarily, you can encourage your husband to let his gifts of wisdom shine. Help him tally up all his years of experience in areas like family leadership, business, even sports and leisure activities. Encourage him to put his practical knowledge to work, serving others who may need guidance in these areas. Let him know he still has many jobs left to accomplish. Now his life's work need not be work, but joy and service to others.

Some dear friends of mine retired early from their employment, though both were still active and full of life. They took an extended vacation in Hawaii, and while on the big island, they went to visit someone who was attending YWAM's Pacific and Asia Christian University. Their friend was gone that day, but since they were there, the couple decided to tour the college anyway.

What they saw excited them so much that they soon found themselves enrolled in a Crossroads discipleship class at the university. That training in turn motivated them to get involved with the university's program for helping other middle-aged and older people who were at crossroads in their lives. For about a year they served happily together in this new ministry. By thus encouraging her husband, the wife gave him a fresh sense of purpose in his later years.

The senior years can also be a time of special openness to one another. Health problems and a limited income need not be causes for fear and stress. They, too, can be tools to draw you together in prayer, dialogue and spiritual growth.

Choose to Love

The one principle that applies in all seasons of life is that you can live according to God's directives and choose to love. Your love for your husband does not have to be a wishy-washy, change-with-the-weather kind of thing. That kind of love turns to mush when things get tough.

Whether you are going through a peaceful or a challenging season with your husband right now, God has a high calling for you. Your love, patience and service will help your husband through hard times. Your enthusiasm and support will also help him, in good times, to become more the man God wants him to be.

Whatever your situation, God can help you be your husband's best friend, a woman of strength, growing in maturity. Isn't that what you really want?